Market Indicators

Also available from
Bloomberg Press

The Trader's Guide to Key Economic Indicators
Updated and Expanded Edition
by Richard Yamarone

Breakthroughs in Technical Analysis:
New Thinking from the World's Top Minds
by David Keller

Technical Analysis Tools:
Creating a Profitable Trading System
by Mark Tinghino

Trading ETFs:
Gaining an Edge with Technical Analysis
by Deron Wagner

New Insights on Covered Call Writing:
The Powerful Technique That Enhances Return
and Lowers Risk in Stock Investing
by Richard Lehman and Lawrence G. McMillan

A complete list of our titles is available at
www.bloomberg.com/books

Attention Corporations

This book is available for bulk purchase at special discount. Special editions or chapter reprints can also be customized to specifications. For information, please e-mail Bloomberg Press, **press@bloomberg.com**, Attention: Director of Special Markets, or phone 212-617-7966.

Market Indicators

The Best-Kept Secret to More Effective
Trading and Investing

Richard Sipley

BLOOMBERG PRESS
NEW YORK

This publication contains the author's opinions, who takes sole responsibility for them, and is designed to provide accurate and authoritative information. It is sold with the understanding that the author, publisher, and Bloomberg L.P. are not engaged in rendering legal, accounting, invest-ment-planning, or other professional advice. The reader should seek the services of a qualified professional for such advice; the author, publisher, and Bloomberg L.P. cannot be held responsible for any loss incurred as a result of specific investments or planning decisions made by the reader.

First edition published 2009
1 3 5 7 9 10 8 6 4 2

Library of Congress Cataloging-in-Publication Data

Sipley, Richard.
   Market indicators : the best-kept secret to more effective trading and investing / Richard Sipley.
      p. cm.
   Includes bibliographical references and index.
   Summary: "A proprietary trader provides an overview of the most popular market metrics devel-oped and used by professionals. The author synthesizes these market signals and provides a run-ning commentary on why they work, and how to use them to trade better and more profitably"--Provided by publisher.
   ISBN 978-1-57660-331-4 (alk. paper)
   1. Investment analysis. 2. Investments. 3. Stock price forecasting. 4. Speculation.
I. Title.
   HG4529.S52 2009
   332.63'2042--dc22

                                                                      2009033055

Mixed Sources
Product group from well-managed forests, controlled sources and recycled wood or fiber
www.fsc.org Cert no. SW-COC-003264
© 1996 Forest Stewardship Council
FSC

Contents

Acknowledgments

Now for the page that's least likely to be read in any book, and yet most important to its author. After this project, I promise that I will actually read other writers' tributes.

Thanks to all the bloggers who share their ideas, insights, and opinions. They have helped me shape my own. Thanks also to all the writers and editors who find good stories and angles and go to the trouble of vigorously fact-checking their material.

Thank you to my colleagues at Boston Private Bank for camaraderie and intellectual debate. And thank you to my clients for the trust they place in me and for our conversations, which remind me of the world beyond my computer screen.

My sincere appreciation to Stephen Isaacs, Ingrid Case, and the rest of the Bloomberg production crew for giving me the opportunity to put my thoughts to paper and for then seeing the project to completion.

My love and gratitude to my parents for their guidance and encouragement through the years.

And finally, my love and thanks to my wife, Stephanie and my children Jack, Ava, and Lila. Yes, the book is done. No, the Cubs haven't won the World Series. We moved to Boston to save you from your father's fate.

Introduction

Beware of geeks bearing formulas.
—WARREN BUFFETT, in his 2008 annual letter to shareholders

SOME PEOPLE SUGGEST that investing is a form of gambling, complaining that they can do as well playing the Pick-3 lotto or betting on roulette. Nothing could be further from the truth. In Las Vegas, the house *always* has the edge. In the stock market, *you* can have the edge, if you wait until conditions are right.

Only poker, in which individuals compete to outwit each other, really compares to investing. At its most basic, poker is about making decisions based on imperfect and incomplete information. Players each hold a few cards that only they can see. Every other player must make educated guesses about who holds what. No one knows which card will be dealt next.

An ability to read other players is the skill that sets master poker players apart. The best poker players notice that the man with the loud shirt plays conservatively; if he bets aggressively, it's likely he has a really good hand. They see that the player in the corner plays with her chips when she's bluffing. In poker, these are known as tells, signals that give observant competitors slightly better odds and help them win more often over the course of many games.

That's the goal of this book. The following pages will describe a variety of signs, or tells, that many market professionals consider. These signs don't replace good, old-fashioned homework—but they will enhance your ability to make better stock decisions over time.

You can observe a lot by just watching.   —YOGI BERRA

If you approach the market solely by doing fundamental research, this book probably won't be of much interest. If you have found your investing niche by concentrating only on technical analysis, this book is not for you. But if you agree that you can learn a lot just by looking around, then you'll likely find some useful nuggets here.

Economist John Maynard Keynes has compared the stock market to a beauty contest, but with a twist. Rather than voting for the prettiest girl, the goal is to pick the contestant *the judges* believe is prettiest. Keynes, who was a very successful stock investor in his own right, read newspapers to learn what others were reading and thinking. He believed that market success requires looking around and observing how other market participants feel and act.

This insight is not unique to Keynes. Professional investors of every era have developed indicators and other rules of thumb that help them navigate naturally chaotic markets. You'll see some of these indicators when excessive fear or greed enters the marketplace. Others arise when well-informed insiders tip their hands and hint at their views of the future. These signals are largely numerical, can be charted, and lend themselves to deep study.

The best and brightest are constantly trying to develop more complex and sophisticated indicators. Careers can be focused on just one signal. Sometimes, however, simple is best. Many of the most reliable indicators have been around for many years, and have stood the test of time. In this book, we'll cover a wide range of indicators, offering the reader a handbook of market "tells."

The Outline

> *I understand now that the financial future is a closed book, that prophecy is usually profitless, and that the best an investor can generally hope to do is identify extremes of sentiment and valuation as they periodically present themselves.*
>
> —JAMES GRANT, in his final *Forbes* column, February 25, 2008

At its core, of course, the future is unknowable. But as long-time market commentator Jim Grant said, investors can better their odds by identifying extremes of sentiment in groups of real people with real foibles and emotions, who buy and sell stocks in the world markets every day.

There are three sets of indicators that may signal opportunity. We will first focus on data that reveals what market participants are *doing*. Normally, there is an ebb and flow in the price and volume of specific securities, and in the market as a whole. A significant, measurable activity spike may suggest market panic or euphoria and, therefore, potential opportunity.

The second section will explore the ways investors, as a group, signal their areas of focus, feelings, and general outlook. At market tops and bottoms, surveys and media coverage reflect investor sentiment. When the media universally portray an issue in a certain way, or when commentators portray the (unknowable) future as clear, it suggests that emotion has trumped rational analysis—and that securities are incorrectly priced as a result.

The third and final section will explore the dynamic between "smart money" and "dumb money." Because of their roles, some people know more than others about specific market sectors. A global grain conglomerate executive knows more about corn crops than does a dentist, for instance. Most of the time, insiders and the general public take similar actions. When their opinions diverge, however, it's wise to follow the insiders. We'll discuss how to find and interpret that moment of divergence.

A Few Warnings

Take what you can use and let the rest go by.

—KEN KESEY

These indicators don't replace economic analysis, or save you the trouble of reading a company's financial statements. In fact, they work best for investors who already endeavor to understand companies, sectors, markets, and their real-world contexts. These indicators are a supplement to the hard work of knowing the stocks you own.

Many of these indicators have been tested for their predictive value, and all fall short in some way. No single or combined indicator will give you a foolproof route to riches.

Instead, I emphasize the importance of considering a broad cross-section of indicators and information to get a sense of what market signals might mean, deciding for yourself how much weight to give any single factor. Take what you can use and let the rest go by.

About Me

Whoever undertakes to set himself up as a judge to Truth and Knowledge is shipwrecked by the laughter of the gods.

—ALBERT EINSTEIN

No book can escape its author's natural leanings. I graduated with degrees in finance and computer science from Miami University in Oxford, Ohio, in 1988, received my MBA at Kellogg School of Management at Northwestern University in 1997, and became a CFA charter holder in 1998.

In nearly fifteen years, I've held positions for ten seconds (once or twice) and ten years (once or twice). I've done paired spreads, warrant spreads, preferred spreads, merger arbitrage, straight longs, and unhedged shorts. I've ridden a stock from fifty cents to sixty dollars and from five dollars to zero. I've sat on cash while everyone around me was minting money. I've gotten into a cab to see a former coworker, who was minting money a year earlier, sitting in the driver's seat.

I'm currently a portfolio manager at Boston Private Bank, where my colleagues and I work with both individual and institutional investors, doing our best to help clients navigate the market.

I've looked at most every indicator out there, considered every nuance I could find, but I also recognize the karmic danger of portraying myself as an expert. I urge you to consider other voices and opinions. Many of the charts in this book come from people who have made interpreting market signals their life's labor. In many ways, this book is an introduction to their work.

Entrepreneur and now-billionaire Mark Cuban wrote that, while he was starting out, he slept on the floor of a shared apartment and ate mustard and ketchup sandwiches. But he figured the more he learned, the better chance he had of beating the competition. Cuban has said that just one good idea from a three-dollar magazine or a twenty-dollar book is a bargain. I hope you find at least one actionable indicator or intriguing concept in the pages that follow. And that you're not eating mustard and ketchup sandwiches. Thanks for reading.

Measuring Investor Actions

As a general rule, the most successful man in life is the man who has the best information.

—BENJAMIN DISRAELI

MONEY DOESN'T FLOW—it sloshes. Like water in an overfull bathtub money moves in waves, as investors process information and balance the competing desires to grow wealth and protect capital. Traders use connections and quick thinking to react to new information, deciding how it may (or may not) affect capital returns. Thoughtful investors try to proactively position portfolios, rather than reacting impulsively to each new data point and market development.

As it sloshes, money creates a variety of measurable results, which signal how investors currently view risk and where they are placing bets. This first section reviews a variety of real-time indicators that point to capital allocation and reveal traders' general levels of risk tolerance. Our first stop: the options market.

Clues from the Options Market

Successful investing is anticipating the anticipations of others.
—JOHN MAYNARD KEYNES

IT CAN BE TOUGH ENOUGH to do well in the stock market. The options market, with its additional layers of complexity, might appear to be an even more challenging place to gain an advantage. Some of the smartest, quickest pros operate in the options market where, like traditional chess grand masters, they are slowly being outsmarted by computer algorithms. But there's no need to battle the options pros or the computers to glean useful information from the options market.

The Basics

At its most basic, an option is simple. It's the right to buy (call) or sell (put) a stock at a stated price (strike) until a certain point in time (expiration date). It's not hard to understand, but it is hard to correctly value.

Though the mathematical specifics are beyond the scope of this book, traders use a few pieces of information to calculate an option's price. These include the risk-free cost of money (due to the underlying loan that's typically present), the stock price, the option's strike price, and the amount of time left on the option. These are all known numbers. An unknown variable, called implied volatility, ties these known numbers together.

An option's implied volatility measures how much the market thinks a stock's value will change—in either direction—in the future. A boring company often has an established business base that probably won't change much. An electric utility, for instance, has locked-in customers who provide a stable demand for product, although a state agency usually limits what the utility can charge. Relatively speaking, a utility's future cash stream is predictable and will probably create a steady price for that utility's stock, and therefore a relatively low implied volatility. Traders will not pay a high price for the right to buy the stock at a much higher level—a right known as a call—because traders think the stock has only a small chance of achieving that higher level.

On the other hand, a technology stock such as Google has a much higher implied volatility. After all, the stock's value has changed significantly in the past, and Google's future business and cash flow is more unpredictable than that of a utility. A call option—a bet that the stock will go up—on Google, therefore, is more expensive than a call option on Consolidated Edison.

For ease of use across option durations, sources state implied volatility in annualized terms. Note that implied volatility does not imply direction; it merely indicates the perceived magnitude of future price changes, both up *and* down.

What is the Volatility Index?

There is no need to independently calculate implied volatility. The Chicago Board Options Exchange (CBOE) introduced the Volatility Index (VIX) in 1993, and it became a popular media topic—albeit, one commentators often discuss oversimplistically. The VIX considers stocks traded on the S&P 500 Index and continuously calculates their implied volatility on a constant, forward-looking 30-day basis. In less technical language, the VIX measures the market's price movement expectations over the next thirty days on the S&P 500. See more detail on the history of the VIX and its underlying calculations, as well as the current VIX and associated values, at the CBOE Web site (www.cboe.com).

WHY INVESTORS AND TRADERS LOOK AT THE VIX

The market essentially serves as a discounting mechanism for investors' collective best guess of what the future holds. When investors disagree more than usual over the path of things to come, prices often bounce around as the market seeks equilibrium. At these moments, the VIX runs at relatively higher levels.

The VIX is also known as the investor fear index, because upward spikes are associated with bouts of market turmoil and uncertainty. Market participants are generally reluctant to put hard-earned cash to work in the market when the future seems murky and unsettled. Other investors may see reluctance as an overreaction to current news events and, therefore, as a buying opportunity.

At relatively low levels, the VIX suggests less disagreement over general stock prices. At these times, the VIX could be called the complacency index. Sustained low VIX levels resemble a quiet and placid lake, smooth as glass. Just a pebble can cause a disturbance. And so it is with the market. If investors expect a quiet market, any news event might cause a stir. Some investors therefore see low VIX levels as an opportunity to sell some stock and reduce market exposure.

STUDYING THE VIX

The VIX is based on data and has been around for many years, so it lends itself to academic study. Many academics are fascinated with the VIX, because it seems to dispel the notion of market efficiency.

In their December 2006 paper "Implied Volatility and Future Portfolio Returns," Prithviraj Banerjee, James S. Doran, and David R. Peterson came to the following conclusions:

- They confirmed that the VIX had a statistically valid track record of forecasting stock market returns over one- and two-month time periods.
- This predictive ability was stronger for highly volatile stocks than for less volatile stocks. The forecasting effect was similar across stock type (growth and value) and company size (large and small).
- The authors were careful to conclude that the VIX was predictive, but did not state that VIX-based trading or investing would lead to market-beating returns.

Another study looked at using the VIX to beat the market. In their November 2007 paper "Can the VIX Signal Market's Direction? An Asymmetric Dynamic Strategy," Alessandro Cipollini and Antonio Manzini looked for a VIX strategy that beat a buy-and-hold approach. They stayed long to the market only when the VIX was at a relative high, and kept their account in cash at other times. They derived relative VIX levels by 1) finding high and low VIX values for a rolling twenty-four-month period, 2) dividing that range into twenty-two equal-value "buckets," and 3) finding the forward three-month market returns for each day, and examining which bucket the VIX was in for each. They found that

- The VIX signals market direction, but is much more useful at high relative levels. Spikes are an especially reliable signal of market direction.
- Low VIX levels have much less predictive ability.
- The VIX had significant skews at its tails. The VIX spent only 0.82 percent of the study period (January 2, 1992 to December 31, 2004) in the highest VIX bucket, and 12.4 percent in the lowest, consistent with the argument that the VIX is better at finding market bottoms than market tops.
- Their constructed model beat a standard buy-and-hold model. The authors felt results would have been even better if the model had allowed more aggressive trading at the highest VIX readings.

A note from market research firm Bespoke Investment Group confirmed the finding that the VIX is more predictive at its highest values than at its lowest. The note discussed insights gathered from a study of more than thirty short-term VIX declines of more than 25 percent between January 1990 and April 2008. The authors concluded that "while sharp increases in the index have historically been a positive for the short-term performance of the market, sharp declines in the index do not necessarily have the opposite effect of negative short-term returns."

USING THE VIX

These and other studies demonstrate that, as a predictor, the VIX is most accurate when it spikes from a relatively high level. This phenomenon can be used to time the market to some degree, particularly in short-term trading strategies, as the VIX considers only the next thirty days. Traders and portfolio managers use the VIX in different ways, with varying levels of conviction, as they seek out approaches that fit their needs and time frames.

We will focus on using VIX spikes to find periods of market dislocation. There are many possible approaches to consider.

MOVING AVERAGES

It can be dangerous to consider any indicator in absolute terms. Many investors tend to find an indicator level that has seemingly worked well in the past, and arbitrarily use that level as a future trigger point. But times and conditions change. It's better to use the VIX by considering it in relation to the trends and trend deviations in its recent past.

One way to look at relative trends and trend deviations is to use moving averages. A 10-day moving average for the VIX is very common, though this can be shortened or lengthened as desired. **FIGURE 1.1** shows a 10-day VIX moving average (solid black line) for 2007, and the circled points at which the VIX spikes by at least 20 percent above those values. Such a relatively large deviation from a given moving average can signify *short-term* fear.

Figure 1.1   VIX 20 percent spikes away from 10-day moving average during 2007

Source: Chart courtesy of StockCharts.com (http://stockcharts.com)

BOLLINGER BANDS

Bollinger Bands, created by John Bollinger, is a charting tool that expands on moving averages and adds a trading range that's based on a security's historical volatility. This charting technique normally uses a 20-day moving average and adds bands representing two standard deviations above and below the moving average. If future volatility matches the 20-day historical volatility, stock price should fall within the two bands 95 percent of the time.

Bollinger explains that the bands' width will expand in a trending market and contract in a sideways market. One can view widening bands as periods of increasing market tension and uncertainty—represented by a more volatile VIX—and tightening bands as times of decreasing market tension and stabilizing VIX values. When the VIX breaks out of a narrow band and heads higher, creating a wider band, one can argue that a new period of uncertainty is underway.

Bollinger Bands changes don't typically occur in a vacuum. Bands usually change width in response to news or other events that affect the market.

Traders use Bollinger Bands in a variety of ways. One approach is to wait for widening bands to develop, then wait for the moving average to crest and begin its decline. The technique won't catch the market's bottom but will increase the probability of finding a point at which the worst of the crisis has passed and the market is rebounding into a new, intermediate-term uptrend.

FIGURE 1.2 shows 2007 VIX data with Bollinger Bands. Periods in which the bands expanded and then the 10-day average ran up and crested are shown in rectangles (roughly March 15, 2007, August 23, 2007, and November 16, 2007).

Note two points circled (February 27, 2007 and August 16, 2007) where the VIX spikes more than 10 percent above the Bollinger Band and is more than 50 percent above the 10-day average. These dates saw marketwide sell-offs—and in retrospect marked good buying opportunities.

DIVERGENCES

Market participants may also use a VIX moving average to find instances where the VIX and the stock market diverge. They might

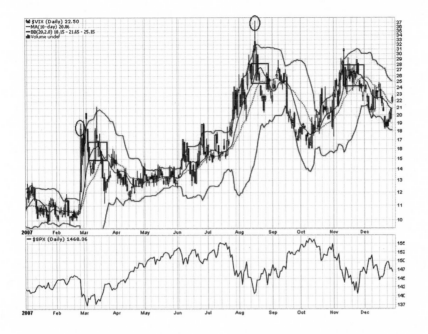

Figure 1.2 VIX with 20-day Bollinger Bands and 10-day moving average during 2007

Source: Chart courtesy of StockCharts.com (http://stockcharts.com)

look for a situation in which the market has made a fresh low and the VIX moving average has not reached a new high. This combination suggests that the general market conditions that spurred the recent market action are starting to moderate.

In Figure 1.2, note that the November market low matches the August low, but that the 10-day VIX line peaked at a slightly lower level. This suggests that market fear was generally dissipating.

In a market downturn, a new low that occurs without a fresh VIX high can be one sign that the market is nearing a bottom. In a market upturn, a new high without a fresh VIX low can signal an intermediate-term top. As we've seen, low VIX levels are less predictive than are abnormally high VIX readings.

PREDICTING VOLATILITY

The VIX uses options to track 30-day stock price volatility expectations, considering investors' collective reaction to current events as well as their emotional responses to the pleasure of gains and pain of losses. Another index, the CBOE S&P 500 Three-Month Volatility Index (VXV), measures the same thing on a longer time frame, charting the three-month implied market volatility of S&P 500 index options. In a sense, this index helps traders anticipate other investors' anticipation.

By comparing the VXV to VIX, market participants can compare the views of shorter-term and longer-term options traders. When the VIX is at a relative high and the VXV is *much* lower, it suggests that longer-term options traders believe that shorter-term traders are having a temporary panic attack, and the current market storm will soon blow over. However, a relatively high VIX *and* VXV suggest that longer-term options traders agree that their colleagues are panicking with good reason (it's been said that those who panic first, panic best), and storm clouds will linger. **FIGURE 1.3** shows this ratio for 2008.

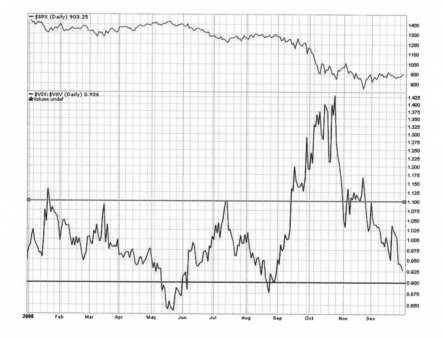

Figure 1.3   Ratio of 30-day to 90-day implied volatility

Source: Chart courtesy of StockCharts.com (http://stockcharts.com)

Bill Luby, on his blog Vix and More (vixandmore.blogspot.com) has suggested that a level of 0.9 suggests a need to decrease stock exposure, and that a ratio of 1.1 suggests that investors increase stock exposure. (The October sell-off blew through the 1.1 buy point. Luby suggests that this indicator will work in many markets over the course of time, but will not do well in a market dislocation.)

Another approach is to wait for extremely high or low ratios to appear and then retreat, waiting until the ratio declines *below* 1.1 in the previous example. Because the VXV indicator is so recent, it will need to be tested through several market environments before its usefulness will more fully be known.

OTHER VOLATILITY INDICATORS

The CBOE offers other volatility indexes, each tracking a different underlying index. The Nasdaq Volatility Index (VXN) measures volatility expectations using options on the Nasdaq 100 index. The Russell 2000 Volatility Index (RVX) tracks volatility expectations using options on the Russell 2000; and the DJIA Volatility Index (VXD) follows the same expectations for the Dow Jones Industrial Average. There are also volatility indexes for several European indexes.

VIX RESOURCES

Many financial data providers offer subscribers the VIX and other volatility indicators and allow users to tinker with various moving averages, Bollinger Bands, and data-smoothing techniques. The CBOE carries basic data on its Web site for free, or with advanced streaming data for a fee. Bloomberg users can find all world volatility indexes by typing WVI <Go>.

Of all the topics in this book, the discussion of VIX and how to use it is the most technical and most open to individual interpretation. The concepts used here are at an admittedly basic level. A blog search on "VIX" will reveal an abundance of individual approaches and commentary on the VIX's usefulness across all market time frames. The blog vixandmore.blogspot.com specifically focuses on the VIX in Bill Luby's market outlook.

Finally, the CBOE Web site (www.cboe.com) offers a comprehensive review of VIX history, its construction methodology, historical data, and real-time readings.

More Options: The Put/Call Ratio

The put/call ratio is the other common indicator to come from the options market. It represents a comparison between all the puts and all the calls purchased on any given day. Known as the aggregate put/call ratio, it facilitates overall market analysis. (Investors can also analyze specific pockets of options activity, in ways discussed later in this chapter.)

There tends to be a balance between investors who are bullish and those who are bearish on specific stocks or the general market. Professionals using options to hedge other positions don't necessarily have an opinion about the direction of a stock or market index. Their strategies don't change much during market extremes, and so have little effect on the relative high and low put/call readings that are the most useful.

Most market participants bet that the market will go up after the market shows a strong advance. (The brain naturally projects recent trends into the future and calls that projection a forecast, a phenomenon called recency bias.) When the market goes up, many participants buy calls, in anticipation of further advances. The put/call ratio goes down. For instance, a given day might show a put/call ratio of 0.9, or 90 puts purchased for every 100 calls. If investors buy more calls in response to an advancing market, the put/call ratio might move to 120 calls to a steady 90 puts, or 0.75.

By the same logic, investors typically buy more puts if they are nervous about a market decline. Some even enter the options market to buy puts as insurance against further market losses. At times of maximum fear and uncertainty, the put/call ratio ratchets up.

Over time, other forces can also affect the baseline put/call ratio. Inverse exchange-traded funds (ETFs), which go up in value when the underlying index goes down, offer an alternative to options for institutions who cannot short stocks or individuals who are unsure about options mechanics. Their growing popularity among investors who can buy puts may have reduced the total number of puts that market participants purchase.

These kinds of structural changes require a flexible approach to the put/call ratio. One possible strategy involves looking for large outlying spikes as indications of market extremes. **FIGURE 1.4** reviews the consolidated equity put/call ratio for 2007 and highlights instances

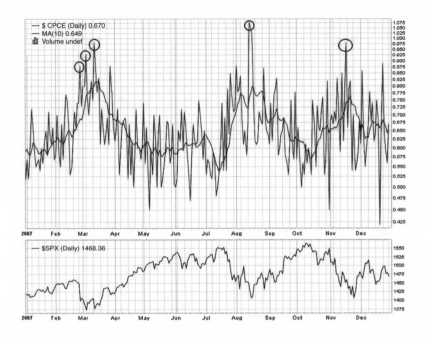

Figure 1.4   Consolidated equity put/call ratio for 2007

Source: Chart courtesy of StockCharts.com (http://stockcharts.com)

when the ratio spiked twenty points or more above its 10-day moving average. As with the VIX charts, it's interesting to note the 10-day moving average, and the points at which it begins rising from a low base. The result is usually more than one day of spiking put volume, before the market finds an intermediate low.

ADJUSTED PUT/CALL RATIO

Another approach involves comparing a short-term put/call ratio with a longer-term put/call ratio to find relative spikes. On his TraderFeed blog (traderfeed.blogspot.com), author Brett Steenbarger creates a relative put/call ratio by taking the 5-day average put/call ratio and dividing it by the 50-day average put/call ratio.

In a quiet market, the recent past would mirror the intermediate past, yielding an adjusted put/call ratio of approximately 1.0. During market extremes, the short-term average would move significantly away from the longer-term average, spiking away from 1.0.

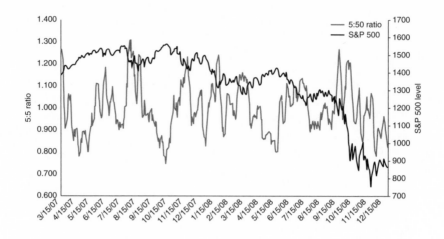

Figure 1.5   Adjusted CBOE put/call ratio

Data: Bloomberg

Steenbarger looked for instances where the 5-day average moved more than 20 percent away from the 50-day average, giving an adjusted put/call ratio of greater than 1.2. Then he checked the market return twenty days later. From January 1, 1998 to December 12, 2007, he noted 188 instances when the adjusted ratio was above 1.2. He found that the Dow Jones Industrial Average gained an average of 2.28 percent (it was up 143 times and down forty-five) twenty days after each spike. The Dow's average 20-day return, by contrast, was 0.39 percent over the same period.

FIGURE 1.5 shows this adjusted ratio for 2007 and 2008. Note that the indicator did not spike above 1.2 at the November 2008 lows; this is because the 50-day put/call average had reached a higher level and would have required an even greater 5-day average to move the adjusted ratio above 1.2.

THE INTERNATIONAL SECURITIES EXCHANGE SENTIMENT INDEX

The International Securities Exchange (ISE) at www.ise.com was the first electronic exchange and has captured increasing volume from traditional floor exchanges. As an exchange, the ISE is in a unique position to track *who* is executing trades, whether these are bullish or bearish bets, and what type of trader is making them.

In 2005, the ISE used this information to create the ISE Sentiment Index (ISEE), which follows the actions of infrequent options buyers, giving the most weight to market participants who enter an options order only when they feel strongly about their predictions and want to make a concentrated bet. Market maker and proprietary firm trades, by contrast, are focused on hedging and don't often make directional bets.

The ISEE Index targets transactions that signal new, opening positions. A new put is potentially more meaningful as a directional bet than is a put bought to close out a previous short position.

According to a study done by the ISE, the Sentiment Index is most relevant when it clusters in abnormally high and low readings. The study concluded that the ISEE can be a good contrary indicator for intermediate market turns.

FIGURE 1.6 shows the ISE Sentiment Index with the 10-day average reading. Note the ISE calculates this index inversely to the normal put/call ratio—it's a call/put ratio. The ISEE value is calculated as (Number of Opening Long Calls/Number of Opening Long Puts) × 100. Low readings correspond with retail investors piling into puts; high readings suggest aggressive call purchases. An investor using this signal might buy at low readings and sell at high readings.

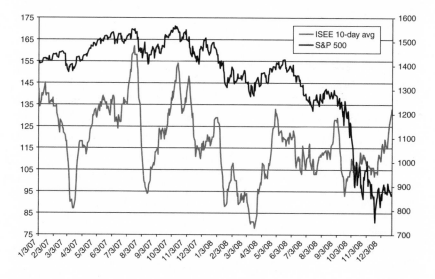

Figure 1.6   ISE Sentiment Index

Data: Bloomberg

Note that during the historic decline in October 2008, the ISEE 10-day reading did not hit new lows. It would seem this type of market wipeout would have strongly driven retail options buyers to buy puts, but this market only reached moderately oversold levels. The ISEE reached the fifth lowest reading (October 23, 2008 with the S&P at 908) since the beginning of 2007, even considering the one-day extremes. Despite the historic sell-off, the ratio suggests that the market didn't reach an intermediate capitulation low.

Another explanation may be found in the VIX readings of the time. They were at all-time highs, reflecting historically expensive options. Investors may have wanted to insure positions by purchasing puts, but couldn't stomach such high prices.

The ISE captures data on a real-time, intraday basis and sells it to short-term traders looking for options-related market insight. Historical information is available on their Web site for free download.

USING OPTIONS DATA FOR STOCKS AND SECTORS

If a person has information or insight he feels is valuable, it makes sense to believe that he would use the options market to magnify the usefulness of that knowledge. Better-informed investors and traders are aggressive buyers of out-of-the-money calls or puts, depending on their convictions. (*Out of the money* refers to options with strike prices far away from the current stock price; these options will gain the most if the stock price moves significantly. Like a lottery ticket, they offer the possibility of huge payoffs that infrequently actually happen.) If an informed trader bought calls in a company he strongly felt would soon be acquired at a substantial premium, the out-of-the money calls would be more expensive than usual, because heavy buying would drive up the implied volatility, and the number of calls outstanding would be greater than normal.

Some studies confirm that these signals are good predictors of future stock returns. In their August 2008 paper "What Does Individual Option Volatility Smirk Tell Us About Future Equity Returns?", authors Xiaoyan Zhang, Rui Zhao and Xing Yuhang studied relative options valuation in predicting future returns. They found that situations in which puts are more expensive than calls tend to predict stock underperformance.

There are several ways to use this signal to sharpen investment decisions. The first is to review the options market for unusual activity. On Bloomberg, the OVI function monitors options spikes. There are several subscription-based services that comb options activity for actionable ideas; two of the better-known services are Schaeffer's Research and OptionMonster. StockPickr.com offers a free, daily service that looks for unusual options volume.

Remember, though, that a spike is a signal—not necessarily a call to action. Sophisticated hedge fund managers are aware of the scrutiny that options activity receives. If a fund has a substantial long or short position, hedge traders may go into the options market and cause an activity spike (by purchasing out-of-the-money calls if they are long, for instance) to attract attention. It's a low-cost, legal way to perhaps nudge the market in their favor.

Analyzing Sectors

Options activity on the most relevant sector exchange-traded fund can lend insight into whether the market is embracing or resisting a sector move. In a behavioral brief on February 14, 2006, the Minneapolis money-management firm Leuthold Weeden Capital Management looked at the sell-off in housing stocks and used the options market to see whether or not the sector was due for a bounce. "Expectations normally track prices," it wrote. "In other words, sentiment towards a group tends to be highly correlated with what the group has done recently. It's when the two diverge that we really have something."

The brief goes on to say that housing stocks, by this measure, were good buys from late 2004 to late 2005, when bullish moves met with heavy put buying. In early 2006, Leuthold Weeden wrote, the market responded to the decline in homebuilding stocks with heavy call buying. Therefore, the study's authors did not think the sector would quickly recover. "Lower prices should scare people," they wrote. "When they don't, look for even lower prices." By the end of 2007, as the residential slide got worse, the S&P Homebuilders exchange-traded fund (XHB) had declined approximately 64 percent, going from $45 to $16.

FIGURE 1.7 examines options activity for crude oil. When oil quickly went from $90 to $120 in the spring of 2008, many felt the sector was in a manic stage and would soon sharply sell off. The options activity in the main oil exchange-traded fund, United States Oil Fund (USO), told a different story.

At the time, the open interest put/call ratio on USO was over 3.0, signaling the market's deep skepticism regarding an oil sector sell-off.

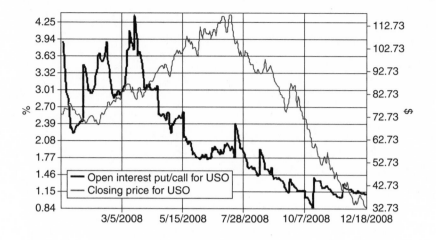

Figure 1.7   Put/call ratio for oil ETF during 2008

Source: Schaeffer's Research

(Almost three puts for each call is a historically high ratio for this ETF.) It signaled bullish sentiment, as oil was seeing heavy selling— yet was strongly climbing anyway.

Sure enough, oil stabilized around $120 through the beginning of summer, then marched upward again to more than $140 per barrel in July 2008. At that time, the USO put/call ratio was under 2.0—still a very high reading, but a big decrease from recent levels. This suggested that investors were wary of continuing to bet against oil, despite the likelihood of a market pullback at some point. As oil came off its boil, the ratio continued to drift down, suggesting that this retreat had a good chance of being more than just a bull market pullback.

Options Resources
ISEE Index data is available at www.ise.com (under Market Data, ISEE Index). For a fee, they also provide an extensive data feed of intraday values, which investors can use to create automated trading strategies. A deep historical view of options data by ticker is available from the Options Clearing Corporation (OCC) at One North Wacker Drive, Suite 500, Chicago, IL 60606. It is not available in a downloadable format, so it can be cumbersome.

RESOURCES

The CBOE published a four-page research note on May 1, 2009, titled "VIX—Fact & Fiction," which can be found at http://www.cboe.com/publish/ResearchNotes/ Research_notes_5-1-09_Issue_2.pdf.

Most academic research papers cited in this book are freely available for download on the Social Science Research Network (SSRN) Web site at www.ssrn.com. SSRN also manages a blog at http://ssrnblog.com, which every week posts the top five papers downloaded from the SSRN eLibrary that week.

One blog devoted to analyzing models and research summaries is www.cxoadvisory.com.

Big Money on the Move

Fear tends to manifest itself much more quickly than greed, so volatile markets tend to be on the downside. In up markets, volatility tends to gradually decline.

—PHILIP ROTH, investor

Never short a dull market.

—WALL STREET maxim

THE OPTIONS MARKET USEFULLY reflects investors' perception of future volatility. But it's also important to look at how stock prices are acting. Is the market calm or turbulent? And what does the current price action reflect?

Before approaching that question, a review of major market participants is in order. Hedge funds nominally controlled almost 1.9 trillion in assets at the end of 2008. These funds generally are graded on a monthly basis and expected to make money most every month while maintaining low volatility: a tall order in a crowded field of very smart, motivated money managers. Hedge funds can move individual stocks and sectors, with a trading style that moves money in and out of positions very quickly.

As a group, pension funds, insurance companies, mutual funds, and sovereign wealth funds contain much more money than do hedge funds, and their influence is much greater and longer lasting. Globally, there was over $60 trillion managed by private institutional investors at the end of 2006. Institutional money can move individual stocks and sectors; it can also move entire markets and indexes, including the $9.6 trillion Wilshire 5000 (as of December 31, 2008), the broadest U.S. market index. We might think of hedge funds as a flashy sports car, one with good acceleration, good handling, a small trunk, and no towing capacity. Institutional money, on the other hand, is more like an 18-wheeler, with poor acceleration and handling, but great storage and towing capacity.

Institutional funds don't like to make frequent changes to their investments. Like a semi truck, they'd rather drive straight down the highway than attempt tight turns. But when they do adjust a portfolio, their huge size makes outsized moves of their buying and selling. Like the fat man doing a cannonball dive, institutional investors make big waves.

Volatility on the Rise

Increased volatility and volume often mean that big institutional money sees a need to adjust asset allocations. Because these organizations have so much money under management, it takes time to complete the adjustments. Their long, slow turns start trends—up or down—that can last for a long time: a matter of months, not days.

In this discussion, market volatility is defined as the number of days the S&P 500 is up or down by at least 1 percent. **FIGURE 2.1** illustrates

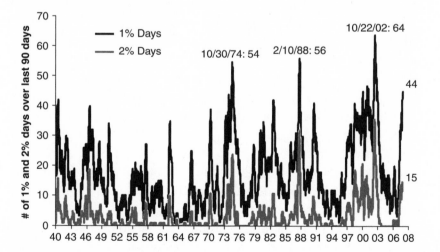

Figure 2.1   Ninety-day running total of 1% and 2% daily market moves, 1940–2008

Source: Bespoke Investment Group

the number of days the market moved 1 percent or 2 percent within ninety days between 1940 and 2008.

Note that the number of sustained, recurring 1 percent and 2 percent swings peaked at times when the market form a meaningful, lasting low. Bad economic news helped form those lows, of course, but what likely unnerved investors even more was the constant whipsawing of prices that made the market seem unstable. Instead of putting money to work in a seemingly schizophrenic market, many investors withdraw from the market and wait for calmer waters. At an extreme, volatility itself—not bad news—encourages investors to abandon hope and dump stocks.

LOPSIDED PRICE MOVES ON LOPSIDED VOLUME

Institutional investors don't typically call a press conference to announce changing investment strategies. By the time reporters notice a trend, much of the trading may be over.

There are ways, however, to gauge market volatility and direction, working long before anyone declares a bull or bear market. Begin by looking for 90/10 days. Lowry Research Corporation (www.lowryresearch.com), a market service in existence since 1938, primarily bases their market analysis on buying and selling pressures on stocks. Their service is geared toward institutional investors, but the main lessons they've learned can help individual investors, too.

After reviewing decades of U.S. market action, the principals at Lowry found that market bottoms are characterized by at least two (and sometimes several) days where at least 90 percent of operating companies listed on the New York Stock Exchange (NYSE) were down on the day, and 90 percent of trading volume was conducted on the bid. Most sellers were motivated, selling stock for whatever price was available.

A market bottom, Lowry has found, is more likely following a few 90/10 down days fairly close together, followed within a few days by a 90/10 up day. These up days, as Lowry defines them, are those where 90 percent of NYSE stocks were up on the day, and 90 percent of trading volume was conducted on the offer, with buyers motivated to purchase at whatever prices sellers make available. The combination suggests that sellers are exhausted, creating a limited supply of stocks for buyers who must then be aggressive to fill their portfolio needs.

Lowry has said that 90 percent down days are often followed by one of the following three patterns:

- A 90 percent up day. One that occurs quickly after the 90 percent down day suggests a sustained, two- to three-month rally.
- A snap-back rally. Without a 90 percent up day, however, such rallies typically last only two to seven days, and are generally followed by new price lows and additional 90 percent down days. Lowry's suggests using the short-term rally as an opportunity to sell stocks.
- A sustained market decline. Without a snap-back rally within a few days after the last 90 percent down day, the market is likely headed for a sustained decline that will produce additional 90 percent down days.

Overwhelming selling that's quickly followed by a day with unusually aggressive buying, Lowry suggests, signals that sellers have exhausted themselves, at least in the intermediate time frame, defined here as between two and three months. Aggressive selling that isn't followed by strong buying suggests that more market weakness is to come.

Lowry's Examination of Market Tops

Market analyst and Lowry's president Paul Desmond and his team, who won the 2002 Charles H. Dow Award for a paper examining market bottoms, have also exhaustively reviewed market history and found a repetitive pattern at major market tops. Near market tops, they argue, the major market *indexes* (Dow, S&P 500) make new highs, but the number of *stocks* making new highs dwindles. Fewer and fewer stocks participate in the market advance.

In each of the fourteen major market tops between 1929 and 2000, an average of only 5.98 percent of stocks made new highs, according to Lowry's research. In the same market tops, an average 22 percent of stocks were at least 20 percent off their highs. Because most portfolios are more diversified than the Dow, an average portfolio might be down by 10 percent on the day the Dow reaches its top.

Lowry's observations on market tops offer the following memorable lessons:

- Tops can take some time to form. (As the Wall Street adage has it, tops are a process, but bottoms are an event.) Even if you were clairvoyant, knowing the date of a major market top would not necessarily spare you from loss.
- Investors should monitor the number of stocks reaching new highs, treating that number as a long-term indicator. In a long-term bull market, a rising percentage of companies should hit new highs. When that number begins to decline in the face of fresh overall market highs, it suggests that caution is in order.

VOLATILITY IN STOCKS AND SECTORS

Top money manager Paul Tudor Jones, who started Tudor Investment Corporation, suggests that, for specific stocks and sectors, volatility often indicates a forming market top, often one that rises exponentially in its final days. That top might indicate market consolidation, he says, or a high that the sector won't reach again for a long time to come. In a January 2000 interview, he said "When you look at the volatility we've had in the past month in the Nasdaq, for instance, every time I've seen volatility like that, I don't care what the market was, whether it was soybeans in '76 or '83 or whether it was silver at the top earlier in 1980 or whether it was some of the biotech stocks at the top earlier in the '90s, when you get that kind of volatility you know that generally it's associated with a top. The best you can hope for if you're long is to look at some type of significant, long-term sideways action where the markets consolidate before moving higher or, generally speaking, allow that those have done their thing and we will have topped for years and years to come. I'm probably more of a subscriber to the latter theory."

It's difficult to quantify, but when you see large (more than 5 percent), closely spaced moves in both directions (perhaps 8 percent up on Monday, 6 percent down on Tuesday, 7 percent down on Thursday, 8 percent up on Friday) it's often an indication that a top is forming. The indication is stronger if stock trends have been in place for a long time, if fundamentals don't fully support a bull market, and if the market is not reacting to a particular bit of news. As with a spinning top that spins steadily and quickly, a wobble may indicate that the end is near. Think of closely spaced volatility in the same way. Many feel that, once a stock or asset class has gone through this type of parabolic rise at the end of a long move, it will take many years to reach new highs. Soybeans and silver, for example, reached highs around 1980 and took nearly twenty-five years to reach new ones.

VOLATILITY—IS IT A BEAR MARKET?

Volatility can also signal that a bear market is at hand. Mebane Faber, the portfolio manager at Cambria Investment Management and keeper of www.mebanefaber.com, looked at days from 1929 to April 2009 on which the market was up or down by at least 2.5 percent. (See **TABLE 2.1**.) He separated the results based on whether the Dow Jones Industrial Average was above (bull market) or below (bear market) its 200-day moving average on the day in question. (He notes that the Dow was above its 200-day average 64 percent of the time during this period, because the market has gone up over time.)

During this period, the market was in "bull" mode 64 percent of the time, with a bull market defined as a period when the market index is above its 200-day moving average. That's nearly twice as often as it was in "bear" mode, which occurred 35 percent of the time. Roughly 70 percent of the highly volatile days occurred when the market was in a defined downtrend, with average volatility nearly doubling during these downward-trending markets. High volatility may suggest a bear market.

Any cluster of highly volatile days may also represent a longer-term bearish signal. Especially coming after a sustained period of rising prices and subdued volatility, this pattern can warn that the market is undergoing a directional shift.

Table 2.1   Returns according to market volatility

DJIA 7/1929–4/2009	Above 200-Day SMA	Below 200-Day SMA
% of the Time	64.31%	35.69%
Average Return (annualized)	10.56%	–2.03%
Median Return (annualized)	13.98%	0.00%
Volatility (annualized)	13.78%	24.59%
Days <−2.5%	27.85%	72.15%
Days > 2.5%	24.24%	75.76%

Source: www.mebanefaber.com

LAST HOUR

If institutions are primarily responsible for the market's longer-term direction, it would be nice to know what stocks institutions are buying or selling. Unfortunately for the individual investor, they go to great lengths to cover their tracks—and for good reason.

The California Public Employees' Retirement System (CalPERS) manages more than $173 billion (as of January 31, 2009) and regularly appears as a top-ten holder of many companies. If its portfolio managers decide to reduce their position in a company in which they own 5 percent of outstanding stock, they will likely sell the position slowly over a few months, during which they will be a constant selling presence. If word got out that they were selling,

- Investors would wonder what CalPERS knew that they did not, assume the worst, and immediately sell, lowering the value of CalPERS' shares.
- Prospective buyers, knowing that one large seller was lurking, would reduce their bid prices and sizes, also lowering the value of CalPERS' shares.
- Short-term traders would short the stock in reaction to the first two facts.

But there are ways to deduce what institutional money managers are doing. One method involves comparing early- and late-day trades.

Imagine that CalPERS wants to sell a hypothetical $5 billion position in IBM. It's unlikely that anyone is ready to buy that much stock at the current price level, so any attempt to sell the position all at once would cause a price decline. Instead, the pension fund instructs its trader to slowly sell into the market, making its best attempt to minimize the impact on stock price. Perhaps the trader decides to sell $100 million of the stock every day for fifty days, with a mandate to sell each $100 million segment by the end of each day.

The trader faces a problem, however, on days when IBM is weak and has no large, committed buyers. The trader might only sell $50 million worth of stock in the first hours of such a day, leaving only the last hour of trading to complete the day's sale. Forced to be aggressive, the trader pushes through the sell order, trading the shares for less than he might otherwise and giving IBM a relative low at the day's trading close. (The opposite might occur if an institution is committed to buying a large amount of stock in a particular order. The trader sometimes will be forced to pay more at the end of a trading day.) By this logic, institutional money may be behind the movement of stocks that end the day at relative lows or highs.

Another explanation for price differences between the market's open and close is the thought that the open is dominated by lesser investors' emotional responses to the previous day's news. The last hour, however, is dominated by more circumspect professionals who have thought through the issues at hand and are completing orders at the close.

Market commentator and portfolio manager Don Hays popularized what he calls the smart-money gauge. Hays' service, Hays Advisory (www.haysadvisory.com), offers a running total—updated daily—that subtracts the Dow's "dumb" money action, which occurs during the first half hour, then adds the "smart" money moves, which occur in the last sixty minutes.

For example, on a given day the Dow might be down 100 points in the opening thirty minutes, but rally 50 points in the closing sixty minutes. The day would increase Hays' running total by 150 points, regardless of what the market as a whole did on the day. A weak close, by contrast, might suggest that institutions are selling stocks to retail buyers. This outlook assumes that the early action represented sales by "weak" holders; the end-of-day trades are from "smart" institutional buyers that often hold positions for the long term. This indicator suggests that a longer-term floor was building, as institutions added to their positions.

This smart-money gauge doesn't indicate short-term buying or selling moments. Instead, its divergence from other market data may signal longer-term opportunities. When the market is generally declining but the smart-money gauge is rising, for instance, it suggests that institutional money managers are consistently building positions.

FIGURE 2.2 looks at 2007 and 2008. The smart-money gauge declined through 2007, as late-day money dried up in comparison to early-morning money, and dramatically diverged from the S&P 500. Sharp increases in the gauge (November 2007 and March 2008) signaled that institutions were aggressively adding to their holdings.

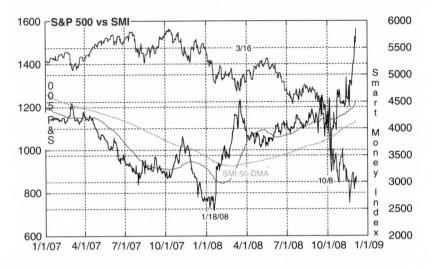

Figure 2.2   Smart Money Index vs. S&P 500 for 2007–2008

Source: Hertler Market Signal

The market met the historic 2008 fall sell-off with significant buying.

MONEY FLOW

Another way to see whether institutional investors are accumulating stock on weakness or selling on strength is to track a stock's money flow. To calculate money flow, take the dollar value of trades conducted on the offer, and then subtract the value of trades conducted on the bid. A declining stock, sector, or market typically shows negative money flow; a rising stock, sector, or market shows positive money flow. Divergence is unusual, but noteworthy. A stock with a declining price but a positive money flow indicates that the stock has plenty of sellers, but that buyers are also aggressively accumulating positions. It suggests that, once the current selling pressure is over, a wellspring of aggressive buyers are ready to take the stock's price back up.

This analysis can be conducted across multiple time frames. An intraday trader might watch the ongoing action between bids and offers to gauge whether the bull or bear story will carry the moment. On a daily or weekly basis, the divergence discussed above can suggest that institutional money, with its deep pockets, is quietly accumulating or dismantling positions.

One publicly available source for this information is the *Wall Street Journal's* daily money flow chart (www.wsj.com under the "Market Data Center" tab), which offers data on various market sectors over daily, weekly, and monthly time frames. It shows money flow in dollar terms and by a ratio of the number of stocks in that sector or index with positive money flow to those with negative money flow. By examining it, one can see aggregate money flow and judge how dispersed or concentrated buying or selling pressure was.

For instance, December 2008 saw a sideways market, as investors digested historically volatile moves in October and November. Under the surface, however, money flow showed that motivated buyers purchased $2.6 billion more of the thirty stocks that comprise the Dow Jones index than were unloaded by motivated sellers. For every one hundred trades on a downtick, there were one hundred and twelve on an uptick. This mild divergence was a mildly positive signal for the market going forward.

USING RATE OF CHANGE

Short-term techniques for observing institutional investors are important but so is watching the longer-term rate of change. Daily observation can take attention away from trends that unfold slowly over time.

Rate of change (ROC) measures how fast the market is moving in a particular direction over a given period of time. The longer the measured time frame, the higher the likelihood that the ROC reflects the true, underlying, sustained trend. Checking a longer trend against a shorter trend can help you decide whether the market's long-term direction supports a current market move.

FIGURE 2.3 shows the S&P 500 for 1999 through 2008. It measures the long-term ROC over fifty-two weeks, and measures the intermediate ROC over thirteen weeks.

The 52-week ROC crossed the zero line on three occasions (squared areas). November 2000 signified the end of a bull market. June 2003 was the beginning of a new bull market, and January 2008 marked the end of that bull run. (Crossover points did not match the long-term tops or bottoms, but did come close.) Areas circled on the 13-week ROC marked times of false hope in a bear market and premature pessimism during a bull market.

Figure 2.3   The 52-week and 13-week rate of change for S&P 500

Source: Chart courtesy of StockCharts.com (http://stockcharts.com)

When the 52-week rate-of-change line crossed into positive territory, it signaled that on balance, over the previous year, the market had displayed forward momentum. Watching the market on a daily basis, it can be difficult to see longer-term trends, which this technique can help reveal. In this case, the data suggested that the bear market's persistent selling had lessened and consistent buying pressure was posed to move the market higher.

RESOURCES

Find market commentary and statistics from Bespoke Investment Group at www.bespokeinvest.typepad.com.

Lowry's main Web site is www.lowryresearch.com. Paul Desmond, president of Lowry's, sometimes publicly comments on the group's findings. A Google Alert (www.google.com/alerts) can be set up to search for "Paul Desmond Lowry's" and Google will send an e-mail with any media mention with this search criteria.

Find investment strategies and outlook from Mebane Faber on his Web site at www.mebanefaber.com.

The *Wall Street Journal* online (www.wsj.com) Market Data Center contains a wealth of market information, including market sector flows and block trades mentioned in the chapter.

Paul Desmond's paper "Identifying Bear Market Bottoms and New Bull Markets" further describes Lowry's market analysis approach. Download this paper, which won the 2002 Charles W. Dow award given by Market Technicians Association, at http://www.mta.org/eweb/docs/2002DowAwardb.pdf.

Fast Money
on the Move

No matter what the markets say, traders are not machines guided by silicon chips; they are impressionable and imitative; they run in flocks and retreat in hordes.

—ROGER LOWENSTEIN, *When Genius Failed*

There are tons of people who are late to trends and adopt a trend after it's no longer in fashion. They exist in mutual funds. They exist in clothes. They exist in cars. They exist in lifestyles.

—JIM CRAMER

LARGE INSTITUTIONS CONTROLLING tens of billions of dollars, as we've seen, tend to move slowly and stick to their investment guidelines. Their substantial resources allow them to diversify by building positions in individual stocks.

Individual investors, by contrast, can move much faster—but may not have the resources necessary to build a diversified portfolio from individual stock positions. They may also share the common human tendency to chase trends at the wrong time, basing their investment timing on the wrong data.

It's possible to spot trends as they're happening, however. A careful look at exchange-traded funds (ETFs), inverse exchange-traded funds, and various types of mutual funds may help reveal what groups of individuals investors are doing and thinking.

Exchange Traded Funds

Perhaps the greatest change in the markets over the past ten years is the explosive growth and increasing popularity of ETFs. These funds trade like single equities, but are actually a basket of stocks, targeted to meet a specific purpose. The most heavily traded ETF, Standard & Poor's depositary receipt (SPDR), for example, is one that emulates the performance of the S&P 500. Instead of buying many securities to create a general market exposure, an investor might buy shares in this ETF, often called the Spider (SPY), which contains shares of all five hundred companies in the S&P 500. As of July 31, 2009, the Spider ETF held more than $70 billion in assets and traded more than 225 million shares each day.

The success of the early ETFs—including the Spider—opened the floodgates for other ETFs that met specific investment needs. If the Brazilian stock market seems attractive but an investor lacks time to research local companies, the iShares Brazil ETF (EWZ) provides broad exposure to that specific market. If the future of alternative energy is bright but an investor lacks the expertise to evaluate competing tec hnologies, the PowerShares WilderHill Clean Energy ETF (PBW) can give good sector exposure.

Even those who hope to profit from market downturns have more than fifty ETFs from which to choose. These ETFs are known as inverse funds. On the S&P 500, for instance, the iShares S&P Inverse Index (SH) is an ETF that goes up in price for every bit that the S&P 500 goes down.

Morningstar (www.morningstar.com), a service best known for tracking and grading mutual funds, also tracks ETF performance and volume. This can help investors identify sectors that are gaining favor—and sometimes discover surprising information.

September 24, 2008, was a day when Wall Street was coming unraveled. The previous week saw seemingly bedrock institutions, such as Merrill Lynch (founded 1914), Lehman Brothers (founded 1850), and AIG (founded 1919), all exit the investment landscape. The government convened a special session to debate a hastily assembled plan for reviving the credit markets. This was the modern-day equivalent of a run on the bank, the most severe test of the financial markets since the Great Depression.

The most active ETFs that day (SPY and QQQQ) track the S&P 500 and the Nasdaq 100, respectively, and always dominate ETF trading. The third ETF, the Financial Select Sector SPDR (XLF), tracks major banks and brokerages. It's no surprise that the XLF was very active during this tumultuous time in the financial industry.

It is surprising, though, that the XLF—the most commonly traded financial industry ETF—did not trade outrageous volume that week. (Volume data is not available on Morningstar, but can be found at charting Web sites such as stockcharts.com or Yahoo! Finance.) Compared to its 50-day average, volume that week was large, but not really abnormal. According to the XLF volume, investors were not stampeding out of financial industry stocks.

That might come as a surprise to anyone who followed media reports that week. CNBC focused exclusively on a bank bailout plan; radio shows debated the merits of various intervention efforts; the president offered the only prime-time speech of his presidency that addressed the domestic economy. Newspapers trumpeted financial sector business failures and credit market problems. Financial Armageddon, they seemed to imply, was upon us. Consider the following *Wall Street Journal* headlines for the week of September 15:

- "Crisis on Wall Street as Lehman Totters, Merrill Is Sold, AIG Seeks to Raise Cash"
- "U.S. to Take Over AIG in $85 Billion Bailout; Central Banks Inject Cash as Credit Dries Up"
- "Mounting Fears Shake World Markets As Banking Giants Rush to Raise Capital"

If that week was not a good time to buy, when was? The whole financial sector had been under extraordinary pressure for the preceding year. **FIGURE 3.1** shows XLF during 2008. What does XLF volume suggest were good intermediate times to buy?

As with the VIX and put/call analysis in earlier chapters, ETF observers can best identify spikes by comparing the current market state to a moving average. It can be dangerous to look for absolute levels; market conditions change over time. A useful or telling level a year ago may be worthless or, worse, misleading today.

Figure 3.1 shows a 50-day moving average on the XLF chart, with daily volume spikes of more than double the average circled.

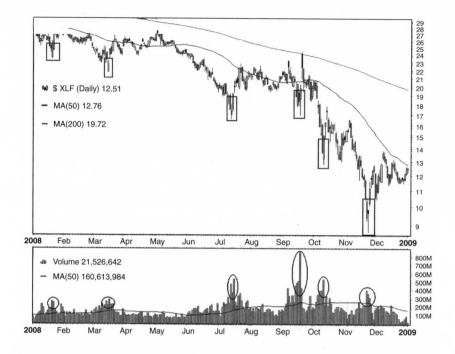

Figure 3.1   Financial Select Sector ETF (XLF) price and volume chart for 2008

Source: Chart courtesy of StockCharts.com (http://stockcharts.com)

These points signaled short-term (one- to five-day) trading bottoms in the XLF.

This data also suggests that the week of September 15, 2008 was a short-term buying opportunity for the financial sector. The last week of September 2008, however, did not represent a buying opportunity.

Notice that volume built over the year, as the financial sector revealed the depth of its problems. The days of greatest volume, however, did not mark the ultimate low. XLF shares plunged below $9 in late November, on volume that was less than half that seen during the September sell-off. A long-term investor could see this as a gradual lessening of selling pressure. Many longer-term bear markets conclude with exhausted sellers and a resulting absence of volume.

Of course, there are many other indicators to consider in analyzing this ETF, including the XLF put/call ratio (available at SchaeffersResearch. com). In **FIGURE 3.2**, one can see investors reaching for downside

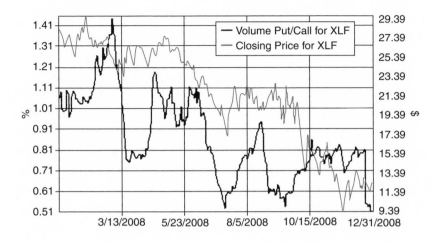

Figure 3.2   Volume put/call ratio for XLF during 2008

Source: Schaeffer's Research

insurance three times: at the beginning of the year, in early March, and in early May, the only three occasions when investors purchased 25 percent more puts than calls. Even those moves didn't suggest that traders were running for the exits. The data implies that many investors, despite the financial sector carnage, were still trying to find a bottom. The sector, which had lost 35 percent for the year by late September, declined another 50 percent when the XLF plunged from $20 to $10 through October and November.

One can repeat this analysis for all the ETFs on the Morningstar list. The results can offer insight into various market sectors and overall markets.

Inverse ETFs

For reasons further discussed in Chapter 4, many individual and institutional investors dislike shorting stocks. A bet that the market will decline may just feel wrong. Investors may not want to put assets in a margin account, as is required to short stock, or be unwilling to pay the higher trading costs often associated with options. Inverse ETFs are a convenient alternative to shorting stocks, and offer a way to profit if a market or sector declines.

But inverse ETFs don't short their underlying stocks. ETFs enter into very short-term contracts (called repurchase agreements, or repos) with investment banks, and use futures to mimic the opposite of the target sector return for that day.

Consider the following example for the key difference. Say the S&P 500 ETF (SPY) is at 100 and goes down 10 percent in one day. It is at 90. The inverse ETF (SH) goes up 10 percent to 110. The next day the market incredibly recovers its losses; the S&P 500 is up 10 points (or 10/90, 11.1 percent) and SPY is back to 100. Meanwhile, SH is *down* 11.1 percent and now trades at $97.78. An investor pays 2.22 percent for a round trip by owning the inverse ETF. The longer one holds an inverse ETF, the greater one's exposure to this tracking error. Inverse ETFs work best for short-term trading strategies.

Even so, inverse ETFs can be powerful trading tools, and their volume changes can offer insight into traders as a group. Consider, for example, the ProShares UltraShort Financials ETF (SKF), which tracks twice the inverse of the financial sector on a daily basis. **FIGURE 3.3** shows its 50-day moving average volume, with days on which the index

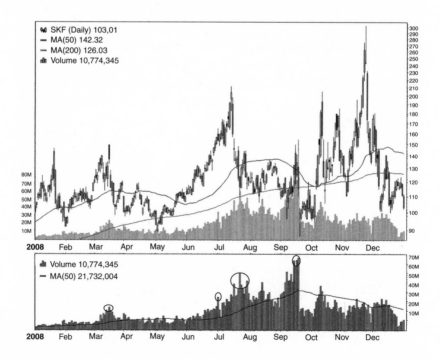

Figure 3.3   Inverse financial sector ETF price and volume chart during 2008

Source: Chart courtesy of StockCharts.com (http://stockcharts.com)

doubled its volume circled. On these days, many traders were chasing trends. Inverse ETF activity often shows spikes around the time a sector or market is ready for a brief rebound, suggesting that retail investors are betting that the sector or market is in for more hard times. To quote an old Wall Street saying, the market will do whatever proves the most people wrong.

ETF Shares Outstanding

Another way of tracking ETF demand is to look at the number of shares outstanding. ETF families such as Barclays and Vanguard adjust the number of ETF shares based on supply and demand. If investor interest in a given ETF increases and people buy and hold more of that ETF, the fund administrator buys more of the stocks underlying the ETF and creates more ETF shares. If investment demand wanes, the fund administrator sells the underlying stocks and reduces ETF shares outstanding.

FIGURE 3.4 shows the number of shares outstanding for the Pro-Shares UltraShort Financials (SKF) just discussed. It shows the peak investment demand (shares being held overnight rather than just passed among traders during the day) in early September 2008. This buildup in demand to hold a bearish financial sector bet occurred at a time when trading demand was above average, but not spiking.

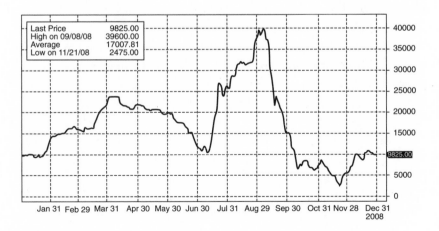

Figure 3.4   Shares outstanding for inverse financial ETF

Source: Bloomberg

The peak SKF price (see Figure 3.3) occurred in late November 2008, during a yearly low in shares outstanding. This suggested that investment demand was minimal and intraday traders dominated the daily action.

Rydex Funds

Before ETFs became popular, many investors found one-stock diversity through the Rydex family of mutual funds. Formed in 1993, Rydex Investments (now Rydex SGI) gave traders an easy, cost-effective way to quickly move between asset classes. It was also an early provider of bearish inverse funds that allowed investors to profit from market declines.

Over the years, Rydex has added new funds that concentrate on a particular sector or market bet. Today, there are over sixty fund choices, including such recent additions as leveraged funds (long and short) for the energy, financial, technology and health-care sectors. Find the entire roster at www.rydexfunds.com.

Investors can shift between any number of Rydex funds without restrictions, making the funds attractive to smaller investors who want both concentrated market exposure and the flexibility to frequently change their minds without penalty.

The Rydex funds report daily on fund assets. Historical report data let investors examine past optimism or despair for a given sector, though with the understanding that Rydex traders typically chase the group's best-performing fund.

Two Rydex funds have a long history of tracking the general market. The Nova fund provides 1.50 times the performance of the S&P 500. The Rydex Inverse S&P 500 Strategy (formerly Ursa) fund is an S&P 500 inverse fund: if the S&P 500 loses 5 percent, the Strategy fund should gain 5 percent.

Consider these funds in relation to one another to find hints about the future. **FIGURE 3.5** shows a ratio of the assets in the Nova funds divided by assets in the Strategy fund, allowing investors to track asset shifts between the bullish Nova and the bearish Strategy. The OEX is Standard & Poor's 100 Index, which contains the largest one hundred companies within the S&P 500. Relatively high readings indicate investor optimism, as more assets have moved into the bullish Nova fund compared to the bearish Strategy fund. Low readings suggest relative investor despair.

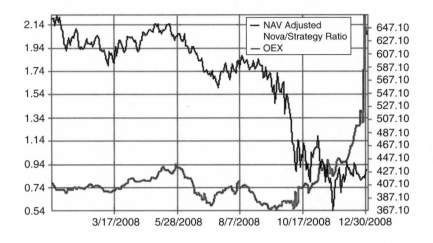

Figure 3.5   Nova/Strategy Ratio

Source: Schaeffer's Research

During 2008, Rydex traders were the most optimistic in late May, before a market decline into the summer, and pessimistic in July, before the rebound into mid-August. The historic fall sell-off broke many historical relationships, and this indicator was no exception. Rydex traders were the most bearish for the year—correctly so, as it turned out. As the year ended, traders piled into the bullish Nova fund (ratio over 2.0), suggesting that the late-year rally was set to fizzle. As it turned out, the OEX declined nearly 25 percent by early March.

Rydex has more than fifteen sector-specific mutual funds and allows investors to freely shift money between them. Many of these sector funds have existed since 1998, giving ample historical data to extend this analysis to individual market sectors. Because there is limited historical data on the inverse (bearish) funds for these sectors, an analysis can't compare bullish and bearish money in the same sector. Instead, it must track the ebb and flow between Rydex funds, which one can do by constructing a ratio of the assets in a sector relative to the assets in all Rydex funds. One can get a sense of investor interest in the energy sector, for instance, by adding the assets in the Rydex Energy and the Rydex Energy Service funds, and dividing the total by the assets in all Rydex sector funds. (The peaks in Rydex energy assets are roughly the same over the years, suggesting a fairly constant asset base.)

FIGURE 3.6 shows the Rydex energy sector price and the Rydex Energy ratio. Even between 2004 and 2008, during the sector's terrific bull run, investor enthusiasm sometimes wavered. At intermediate peaks, more than 35 percent of total Rydex sector fund assets were concentrated in energy. At these points, energy stocks had generally enjoyed heady recent gains. As prices increased, the sector attracted more assets.

When energy prices faltered—in the midst of what we now know was a generational bull market for energy—investors quickly questioned their reasons for investing in that sector. In a few months of energy stock underperformance, assets in the Rydex Energy fund declined by nearly 80 percent as investors lost enthusiasm for that market sector.

Expanded SentimenTrader sector analysis, which includes total assets in ProShares ETFs, track leveraged bets, both long and short. We see a pattern similar to that of the Ryder funds.

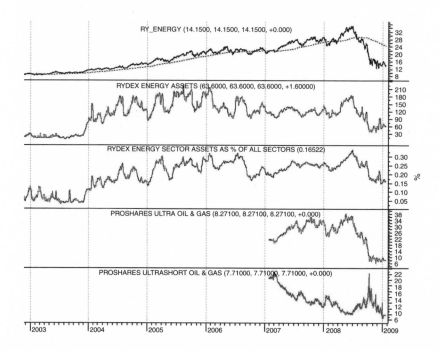

Figure 3.6   Rydex and ETF fund flows for energy sector, January 23, 2009

Source: SentimenTrader.com

This type of analysis can be conducted across all the Rydex sectors. For information on the Rydex mutual funds, visit www. rydexfunds.com. SentimenTrader.com and DecisionPoint.com both offer Rydex fund data.

Over-the-Counter Volume

Large firms list their stocks on one of two exchanges: the New York Stock Exchange (NYSE) or the National Association of Securities Dealers Automated Quotations (Nasdaq), which lists a combined total of nearly forty-five hundred domestic and foreign companies. Firms must meet listing requirements, which include being current on SEC filings and meeting a minimum market capitalization, before trading on either exchange.

If a firm does not meet requirements for the NYSE or the Nasdaq, it may qualify for listing on the NYSE Amex, which has somewhat laxer requirements. Firms that don't meet the standards of these three main domestic exchanges can consider two other, over-the-counter (OTC) exchanges: the Over-the-Counter Bulletin Board (OTCBB) and the Pink Sheets.

A few large firms trade on these small exchanges. Switzerland-based Nestlé is one; as a foreign firm, it didn't want the expense of meeting U.S. Sarbanes-Oxley compliance. Generally, however, the OTC exchanges host the smallest and most speculative companies, which may then move to a bigger exchange as they grow. (Berkshire Hathaway, which went from trading for just a few dollars on an OTC exchange to trading at $96,600 per share on the New York Stock Exchange at the end of 2008, is one of the best-known success stories.)

Most small firms on the OTC exchanges, however, never grow enough to move to the NYSE; they are acquired, or they go out of business. Nor do they attract institutional investors, who are unlikely to own stock in a company with a market capitalization of less than $100 million. The OTC exchanges are retail investors' territory.

Investing in one of these small companies is a bit like buying a lottery ticket. The buyer may hit big—but the chances of doing so are very small indeed. By looking at the dollar volume traded on the OTCBB and the Pink Sheets, one can see just how lucky—and risk tolerant—retail investors are feeling.

FIGURE 3.7 shows a multiyear chart for dollar volume in OTC stocks. Note the massive increase at the very top of the Nasdaq bubble,

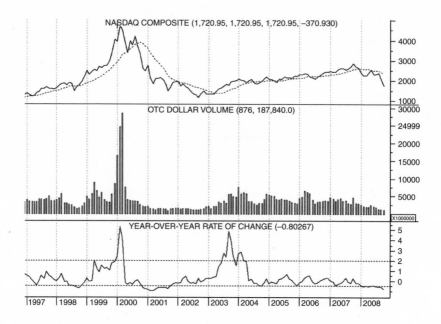

Figure 3.7   Over-the-counter dollar volume, November 8, 2008

Source: SentimenTrader.com

formed in the early months of 2000. Urged on by the success of the likes of tiny Pets.com, which reached a peak valuation of more than $350 million before its November 2000 liquidation, investors piled into small, speculative stocks.

When the dot-com bubble popped, OTC stock volume plummeted. By 2002, many investors had lost money, and their risk tolerance approached zero. Normal dollar volume might have been about $3 billion per month, but shriveled to less than $1.5 billion in 2002. As the broad market rallied in 2003, OTC stock volume gradually returned.

Fund Flows

A branch of study called behavioral finance reveals that the mind seeks pleasure and avoids pain in ways that generally lead to poor investment decisions. Humans have an unfortunate knack for getting out of the market at the bottom when all the news is bad and stocks have generally suffered, and back in towards the top when the news is generally good and the coast seems clear. This tendency prevents many investors from maximizing returns.

In an April 2008 column, MarketWatch.com columnist Chuck Jaffe looked at long-term market returns and compared them to average investor experience. The difference was striking. Citing research from Dalbar Financial Services, Jaffe wrote that over the previous two decades the market returned an average 11.8 percent per year. However, because of ill-timed market entrances and exits, the average investor got an average 4.3 percent annualized return over the same time frame. A buy-and-hold investor could turn $10,000 into $85,094 over twenty years; an "average" investor would have $23,210. That's the difference between a comfortable retirement and a more difficult one.

Watching ETF and Rydex fund flows can help spot times that the broad investor's judgement have been clouded by these emotional blind spots. Being aware of extremes in flows in and out of funds can help take advantage of these natural investor sentiment changes.

RESOURCES

Morningstar is best known for analysis of mutual funds but also provides a wealth of ETF information on its Website, www.morningstar.com.

Bernie Schaeffer and his team at www.schaefferresearch.com features many market and option tools, and the Quotes & Tools tab on the site offers several monitoring charts. This chapter employed the volume put/call ratio as well as the Rydex Nova/Strategy ratio.

Rydex funds and some historical data are available at www.rydexfunds.com.

A subscription site, www.sentimentrader.com, offers an array of indicators and analysis. This chapter examines Rydex ratios, over-the-counter volume, and AMG mutual fund flows. As of press date, the site offers a two-week free trial for new subscribers. The proprietor of the site, Jason Goepfert, maintains a blog called Sentiment's *Edge* at sentimentrader.blogspot.com and writes for minyanville.com.

Other resources for fund flow information include AMG Data Services (www. amgdata.com) and TrimTabs (www.trimtabs.com). Both are subscriber services, but occasionally their insights are mentioned in the media.

Follow the Money: Cash, Debt, and Shorts

There's nothing wrong with cash. It gives you time to think.

—ROBERT PRECHTER JR

REAL ESTATE AND ARTWORK and other collectibles may appreciate, but it can be tough to get your money out of them. For that, you need one or more of the three types of liquid investments: stocks, bonds, and cash. Market strategists (more on them in Chapter 9) focus on these three basic categories, varying their allocation slightly between stocks and bonds based on their market outlook. Cash—such as that kept in money market accounts—is usually an afterthought.

Some investors think that "cash is trash." It yields less than a bond and lacks the growth possibilities enjoyed by a stock. And it's true: nobody ever got richer by sitting on cash.

Of course, nobody ever went broke sitting on cash, either. Bonds occasionally default. Stocks can go to zero. When times get tough, cash looks great.

Seth Klarman, founder and manager of the successful Baupost Group and author of *Margin of Safety*, writes that he sometimes holds a great deal of cash in clients' accounts. He explains that owning stocks he doesn't *really* like removes his ability to take advantage of future bargains. "Maintaining moderate cash balances or owning securities that periodically throw off appreciable cash is likely to reduce the number of foregone opportunities," he writes.

Klarman is an exception. Most investors raise cash after stocks have significantly declined. The cash cycle looks like this:

- **Market bottom:** Cash levels are at historically high levels.
- **Market rising:** Cash levels decline as investors slowly put cash back into the market.
- **Market rising some more:** Cash is at normal to low levels. Some investors begin to borrow, taking on margin debt to buy more stock. They push the market higher.
- **Market topping:** Investors have deployed all investable cash, and margins are at historically high levels.
- **Market declining:** Margin debt drops slowly, as traders are unwilling to believe that the good times are coming to an end. Smart investors realize that the bull market is showing wear and aggressively reduce portfolio leverage.
- **Market downturn:** Leveraged investors feel heavy losses; they sell holdings to pay down margin balances. Selling and deleveraging combine to push the market lower. Investors who didn't use margin debt grow nervous and dismantle their existing equity positions, with many returning to the safety of cash.
- **Bottom:** The cycle is complete. Cash levels are high, margin levels are low, and investors such as Seth Klarman are using cash to purchase bargain securities.

This chapter will consider this cycle, as well as the signals an observant investor might glean from analyzing cash levels, margin debt, hedge fund exposure, and short-selling levels. From cash on hand to margin debt outstanding, an investor can gain market insight by knowing the sources of potential buying and selling. An advancing market needs cash and available margin debt. A declining market is often marked by the opposite: little investable cash and an abundance of margin debt in accounts with dwindling value.

Cash

Many traders believe that mutual funds typically hold large cash balances at market bottoms, and small balances at market tops. In his October 2004 paper (which won the Charles H. Dow Award), Jason Goepfert of SentimenTrader.com discussed this common perception.

First, he reviewed why a mutual fund manager may want a low cash level:

1. The manager believes the market will go up.
2. The fund can use options and futures and has no need to hedge with cash.
3. Fund rules require full investment. Fund investors want equity exposure and are paying the manager to pick stocks, not make an asset allocation decision.
4. Holding cash decreases the chance of beating the benchmark in a rising market, a concern when index funds are proliferating.
5. There are no good alternatives to cash.

Goepfert goes on to suggest that higher interest rates lead to higher cash levels, because a higher return on cash makes it a relatively more attractive alternative to stocks.

The increasing popularity of ETFs and the use of derivatives, however, makes it difficult to gain insight just by looking at mutual fund cash levels. Instead, analysis must occur in a place where investors switch in and out of cash based solely on their investment outlooks, and where cash measures latent buying demand for stocks, without serving as an investment in its own right.

The Rydex funds are that place. In Rydex funds, cash accounts only serve as placeholders, marking time until a trader creates a deployment strategy. Investors can gauge the market's appetite for cash—and potential lack of enthusiasm for other investments—by considering the percentage of total Rydex assets held in the Rydex money market fund. **FIGURE 4.1** shows this ratio.

Sharp cash-level increases may signal that something caused investors to liquidate positions and move to the safety of cash. For instance, in the early months of 2005, cash levels rose from 24 percent to 34 percent of total Rydex assets. That move occurred as rising oil prices weighed on the market. Oil had moved to more than $55 a barrel, and there was general concern that OPEC could not use spare capacity to reduce the price, as the cartel had in the past. High oil prices, investors believed, could slow the economy. Over time, news of rising corporate profits outweighed energy concerns and the market rebounded.

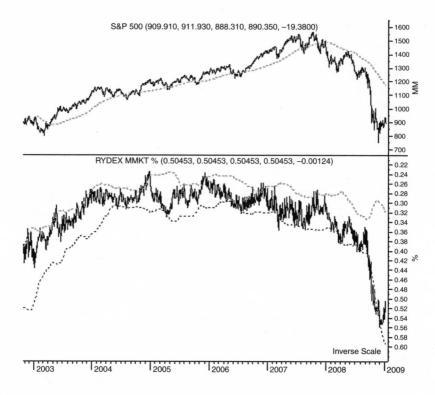

Figure 4.1   Percentage of Rydex assets held in cash

Source: SentimenTrader.com

Cash levels went down more gradually between 2003 and late 2004. As the 2001–2002 bear market subsided and the S&P 500 trended higher, investors gradually increased their equity exposures.

MONEY MARKET VERSUS MARKET MONEY

There are many reasons to have money in a bank account or money market fund. Everyone needs ready money to pay bills and cover emergencies. Beyond that need, however, investors can expect a higher return on long-term, investable cash when they buy bonds or stocks. Comparing sidelined cash to total stock market value can give investors a sense of whether the market is undervalued, as indicated by cash values that stay unchanged while overall market value declines. It can also demonstrate investor confidence levels, as many traders tuck money into bank accounts in anticipation of poor stock market performance. At those times, total cash levels rise.

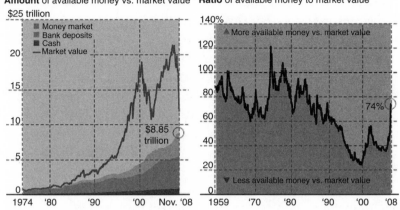

Amount of available money vs. market value   Ratio of available money to market value

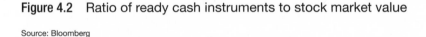

Figure 4.2   Ratio of ready cash instruments to stock market value

Source: Bloomberg

The chart in **FIGURE 4.2** looks at relative monthly cash levels and monthly market values between 1959 and November 2008. As seen in Rydex fund data, investors often successfully deploy cash as equities recover from a bear market. As the stock market goes down, by contrast, traders sell stocks and raise cash.

This chart shows that, in the mid-1970s, cash levels peaked in relation to market value, as many investors abandoned stocks after the brutal 1972–1973 bear market. Note the spike in 2000, when investors allocated cash to mutual funds focused on Internet stocks, which had shown spectacular returns. The ratio of cash to market value rose after the dot-com bubble burst and cash returned to the bank vaults.

With monthly updates, this data offers a very-long-term view of investor risk tolerance, and may indicate points at which money reenters the market after a downturn.

HEDGE FUND CASH

Hedge fund managers are paid to make money. They typically earn 2 percent of funds under management and 20 percent of returns in a combination often known as "2 and 20." The manager of a $1 billion fund producing a 12 percent return collects $44 million for successfully managing that money—and for attracting additional investors.

Hedge funds offer managers the possibility of high pay, but unique pressures, too. For this premium price, hedge fund investors have higher expectations than do many other investors. They demand consistent, positive returns and generally low volatility, no matter what the markets are doing, an approach known as "absolute return." A typical mutual fund, by contrast, measures "relative return," or return relative to a given index or other benchmark.

If a hedge fund loses money, managers lose their return-based compensation: 20 percent of a loss means a performance fee of zero. Furthermore, managers don't collect future performance fees until the fund recovers past losses. A hedge fund that loses money for more than a few months may not survive. Investors leave in search of better returns. With no performance-based compensation or bonuses, top employees may also depart for greener pastures.

High expectations and low loss tolerances force hedge fund managers into a constant awareness of short-term performance. In the aggregate, hedge fund managers often act very much like Rydex traders.

To make money under these conditions, hedge fund managers conduct top-notch research in search of small market inefficiencies and inventive ways to exploit them. Maybe, for instance, a particular company's convertible bonds are slightly mispriced in relation to its stock price. The inconsistency is slight, perhaps enough to produce a return that's a slender 2 percent over money market rates.

After fees, that would leave little for investors, and even less to compensate fund managers. So hedge funds use leverage to magnify their returns. A hypothetical $200 million hedge fund could borrow $800 million at 4 percent from their brokerage fund, putting a total $1 billion to work in their 6 percent return strategy. Assuming all goes well, the fund makes $60 million on its investments, pays $32 million interest, and returns $28 million (before fees) to its investors. With leverage, a 2 percent edge turns into a 10 percent outperformance. Instead of a 4 percent return on cash, this hedge fund offers investors an attractive, relatively stable 14 percent.

When times are good, hedge funds are quick to borrow money and extend positions, seeking to amplify their returns. When the market tops and turns lower, hedge funds move with equal speed to liquidate positions and reduce loan balances, rather than pay interest on loans used to hold money-losing assets. When the market is near its bottom, hedge funds are risk averse. They barely use their credit lines, changing their focus from reaching for every penny of profit and focusing instead on keeping what they have.

In the 1990s, leverage was a big part of the rise of Nasdaq-listed technology and Internet companies. When the market turned, the concentration of borrowed money in these stocks almost guaranteed their ferocious losses.

In 2007, leveraged money likely piled into commodities. Between January 2007 and July 2008, the commodity index (CRB) increased by more than 50 percent. Oil shot from $60 a barrel to $140 a barrel. Life was good for a speculator using leverage. When the market dipped, however, commodities took a hard, hard fall. Oil went from $147 to under $40 in just a few months. Other commodities endured similar declines. (See Chapter 12 for more detail on this phenomenon.)

One could argue that economic forces accounted for these moves, but it's difficult to believe that such enormous price changes were entirely due to normal changes in supply and demand. In each example, debt levels reached a high on the run-up, then fell as prices dropped. The asset class with the greatest increase in each cycle also experienced the sharpest decline.

Individual hedge funds closely guard their trading strategies, making it difficult to spot trends in the 1.9 trillion global industry. Observers can watch indirect indicators, however, including the amount of credit available at Merrill Lynch/Bank of America, Goldman Sachs, and other brokerage firms that loan money to hedge funds. Every month, the NYSE reports on total free credit, a number equal to total brokerage margin credit lines, less the amount already extended to clients.

FIGURE 4.3 shows the cycle on which hedge funds use credit. At the 0 level in the second pane, hedge funds are using half of the available credit to them. A large negative number reflects maximum leverage; a large positive number shows minimum leverage.

Hedge funds deployed increasing leverage from mid-2006 into mid-2007, when the S&P 500 reached 1350. Hedge fund credit then contracted dramatically in late 2007, many analysts believe, though hedge fund secrecy makes it difficult to be sure. The cause is difficult to know. Hedge funds may have voluntarily deleveraged by selling assets in the face of losses, or they may have sold assets in

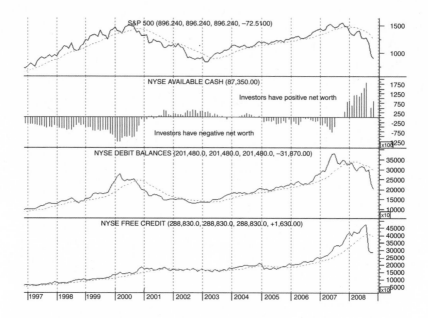

Figure 4.3   NYSE available cash and free credit

Source: SentimenTrader.com

response to margin calls, in which banks demand immediate repayment. The effect, however, is clear. Available credit piled up throughout 2008, and hedge funds sold what assets they could. Though it wasn't the root cause, this selling exacerbated an increasingly severe bear market.

As an indicator, free credit can't help traders find market tops and bottoms. It does, however, give clues to the identity of the buyers behind a rising market. Investors should proceed cautiously in a rising market that's also seeing decreased free credit. When traders use debt to buy stock, that money will quickly exit the market at the inevitable market decline. Free credit levels can also point to sustained, forced selling, as well as to the presence of sustained buying that's pushing asset prices higher.

MARGIN DEBT

Traders can also track leveraged buying by reviewing NYSE margin debt. **FIGURE 4.4** shows year-over-year changes in margin debt. Sharp increases in margin debt presage significant market rallies; decreasing margin levels suggest a market that is more vulnerable to sell-offs.

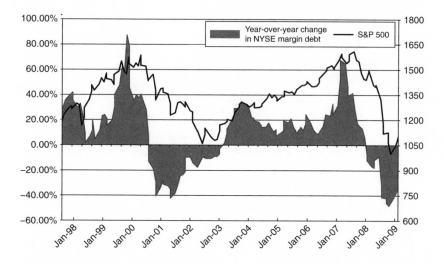

Figure 4.4   Year-over-year changes in margin debt in relation to S&P 500 levels

Data Source: Bloomberg

Something Borrowed, Something Sold—The Short Trade

A trader who executes a short trade borrows stocks from a broker, sells them in the marketplace, collects the money, and promises to return the stock at a future time. If the shorted stock pays a dividend, the short seller pays that dividend. Brokers typically monitor short sellers' accounts, to ensure that they are able to cover their obligations. (Short sellers bet that the market will fall, so many long-term investors and company managers don't care for them, though they play a vital role as the market's devil's advocate.)

Short sellers run two strategy-specific risks. First, they profit only if stock prices fall, allowing them to sell a stock position now for more than it costs to buy an identical position in the future. The strategy can go drastically wrong if the market rises, forcing the short seller to pay more—sometimes much more—to buy back already-sold stock. Theoretically, there is no limit on potential losses. A short seller could be utterly wiped out in a strongly advancing market.

Second, a short seller's broker can ask for the stock back at any time. The move, known as a buy-in, happens when a broker's customer (who unknowingly lent the position) sells the position themselves, forcing the broker to retrieve the borrowed stock. Customers typically sell stock when the market is rising—just when it's most expensive for a short seller to replace the borrowed equities.

The market is littered with stories of short sales gone wrong. Midway Games (MWY) is one example. The company is best known for their Mortal Kombat video game series, but couldn't develop other hit games. The company took on debt, changed CEOs, missed launch dates, and reported quarter after quarter of continuous losses. The end seemed clear, and short sellers increased their positions.

As Midway struggled, Viacom founder and CEO Sumner Redstone increased his position in Midway Games, going from 20 percent to more than 80 percent ownership. Shorting Midway got harder, in spite of its horrible earning reports and deteriorating balance sheet. Perhaps Redstone was right and there *was* real value in the Midway franchise. In any case, Redstone's growing ownership stake meant that fewer and fewer shares (of the total outstanding) were available to short.

FIGURE 4.5 shows short seller interest in Midway Games during 2005 and 2006. The heavy line represents the short interest ratio, or the number of days it would take a short to cover the position given recent stock volume. The bottom panel shows the actual short sales outstanding, with a peak as the stock declined in spring 2005. The % Float in the upper right-hand corner points to the amount of available stock that brokers have loaned out. Anything over 10 percent is

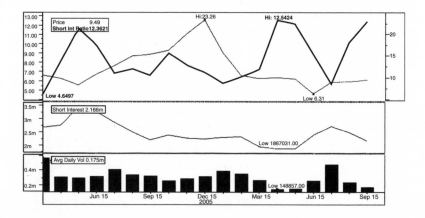

Figure 4.5   Short interest in Midway Games stock

Source: Bloomberg

generally considered a high number. At nearly 30 percent, brokers can still lend out shares, but short sellers take a higher risk that their positions will be called in. If short sellers will take that risk, the stock may be very vulnerable—or it may be poised for explosive gains when short sellers are proven wrong, and must repurchase the stock.

The stock started climbing with Redstone's purchases, going from $10 to $14. Rumors flew of a "short squeeze," which occurs when stockholders move shares from a margin account to a cash account, preventing brokers from lending those shares. Short sellers considering the stock's unchanged fundamentals held tight to their positions, if they could.

The stock continued its run. Many short sellers covered and closed their positions at $22, a loss of more than 100 percent on what had looked like a sure thing. The stock ultimately came close to $25, up from $8 just six months earlier.

Then Midway stock plunged back down, slicing through $15 within a few weeks and landed back at $8 within a month or two. In December 2008, Sumner Redstone sold his stake for $0.0012 per share plus assumed debt; he took a reported $800 million tax loss. The short sellers had correctly gauged Midway's future—but many still got their clocks cleaned.

To take a short position in the face of possible disaster, short sellers must *really* believe a stock will lose value. Extra research gives them the conviction they need to sell a stock short, even when they know that another Midway scenario could unfold.

In an October 27, 2008 research note, brokerage firm Alliance Bernstein looked at what short selling data reveals. They found that

- A large increase in short sales during the past twelve months is a good predictor of stock underperformance for the upcoming twelve months. An absolute level of short sales is less predictive.
- Highly shorted stocks that show subsequent large increases in short seller interest were particularly prone to price declines.

As one might expect, stocks that get the most attention from short sellers tend to underperform the broad market. Traders can get more insight into the day's most popular short ideas at www.locate-stock.com, which also lists the top five most requested "locates" for the day. A locate request asks a broker to find shares available for borrowing. Many stocks that are already heavily shorted are either on a "hard to locate" list (traders must pay a higher fee to borrow these shares) or a "do not borrow" list. There is also a "threshold list," released daily by exchanges, listing stocks that are so heavily shorted that traders must take extra effort to get permission to short them. Some traders use these lists to see which stocks might get squeezed.

FUEL FOR A REBOUND

Just as high margin levels can forecast latent selling pressure if the market heads south, short-seller interest can reveal future buying demand if stocks start to head up. Be careful when determining the reason for a company's stock advance; it may be the result of short sellers closing trades, and have little to do with company performance.

Shorting has become more popular over the last few years, with rising hedge fund assets and the advent of mutual funds that allow short selling. **FIGURE 4.6** shows the number of shares shorted on the NYSE since 2000. That figure rose from eight billion in 2006 to more than 16 billion in 2008. While the increased popularity of

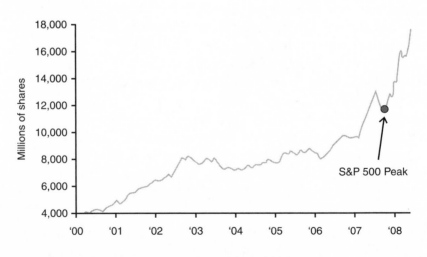

Figure 4.6   NYSE short interest ratio, 2000–2008

Source: Bespoke Investment Group

hedged strategies has made this indicator somewhat less predictive, the number of shorts still represents the market's downside cushion, as many of these shares are eventually repurchased.

SHORTING ETFs

Rather than short specific stocks, investors can make a negative sector bet by shorting an ETF instead. Investors miss the hoped-for pleasure of riding a stock down to a price of zero, but also pass on the risk that a stock's value will double or triple in the near term. Because they are a collection of many stocks, ETFs are not as volatile as individual securities.

Some traders take long positions on a few stocks they think will do well, but short an ETF for that industry sector. A position that's long on Target (TGT) and Abercrombie & Fitch (ANF) but short on the Retail HOLDRs ETF (RTH), for instance, would make money if Target and Abercrombie & Fitch performed *relatively* better than the whole industry.

Looking at short sellers' interest in ETFs also gives a good sense of how negative investors are on the industry an ETF covers. **TABLE 4.1** shows a list from Bespoke Investment services from July 30, 2008, listing ETFs by the percent of outstanding shares shorted in each. (It's possible to short more than 100 percent of shares, because market makers can create more ETF shares if necessary.)

In a market rally, heavily shorted sectors often do well because short sellers quickly close positions by buying stock to cover their short trades if the market moves against them.

Traders can also look at heavily shorted specific stocks that have the potential to move up strongly in a short period of time. This potential is enhanced if a large institution or insider buys the stock to show confidence in the company and/or to take stock out of circulation for borrowing purposes. A heavily shorted stock can resemble a theater with a fire hazard problem. Everyone knows the danger and the fact that the exit door is fairly narrow and limited; but the movie is just too tempting. If smoke appears (in the form of the stock rallying), the temptation for the short seller is to make it to the exit (cover the short) as quickly as possible. Insider buying is one way of throwing a smoke bomb into this hypothetical theater. We will revisit this theme in Chapter 15.

Table 4.1   ETFs with highest short interest, July 30, 2008

ETF	Name	Price	YTD % Change	Short Interest	Short Interest as % of Shares Outstanding
XRT	SPDR S&P RETAIL ETF	29.96	−10.73	37464520	675.04%
RTH	RETAIL HOLDRS TRUST	89.05	−4.61	38319476	464.65%
KCE	KBW CAPITAL MARKETS ETF	45.67	−31.77	6910397	282.06%
ONEQ	FIDELITY NASDAQ COMP INDX TS	91.39	−12.05	2429523	242.95%
IWM	ISHARES RUSSELL 2000	71.61	−5.68	301105075	237.18%
RKH	REGIONAL BANK HOLDERS TRUST	103.66	−20.58	4516652	235.73%
KRE	KBW REGIONAL BANKING ETF	30.09	−18.85	25313188	216.35%
USO	UNITED STATES OIL FUND LP	99.14	30.86	24763860	180.76%
IYR	ISHARES DJ US REAL ESTATE	61.80	−5.94	51802939	173.54%
PMR	POWERSHARES DYN RETAIL PORTF	15.04	−4.02	1715590	142.97%
SMH	SEMICONDUCTOR HOLDRS TRUST	28.01	−13.71	31861179	131.46%
XLB	MATERIALS SELECT SECTOR SPDR	40.47	−2.95	35495948	126.00%
OIH	OIL SERVICE HOLDRS TRUST	195.16	3.25	13066099	115.54%
XHB	SPDR S&P HOMEBUILDERS ETF	17.06	−11.84	32069951	113.32%
XOP	SPDR S&P OIL & GAS EXPLORATI	54.85	5.48	4376688	91.18%
XLE	ENERGY SELECT SECTOR SPDR	75.58	−4.75	70087106	84.22%

Table 4.1   ETFs with highest short interest, July 30, 2008

ETF	Name	Price	YTD % Change	Short Interest	Short Interest as % of Shares Outstanding
IBB	ISHARES NASDAQ BIOTECH INDX	87.15	7.35	18091514	81.49%
TLT	ISHARES LEHMAN 20+YR TREAS	90.66	−2.56	16686885	78.71%
FXB	CURRENCYSHARES BRITISH POUND	198.75	−0.44	426714	77.58%
IYT	ISHARES DJ US TRANSPORT AVG	91.21	12.26	5109168	76.83%
NUCL	ISHARES S&P GBL NUCLEAR ENGY	46.61	-	65856	65.86%
OIL	IPATH GOLDMAN SACHS CRUDE	73.25	30.45	1565905	61.50%
XLY	CONSUMER DISCRETIONARY SELT	28.64	−12.42	23072644	61.04%
UTH	UTILITIES HOLDRS TRUST	125.19	−8.10	658965	59.80%
EWW	ISHARES MSCI MEXICO INVESTAB	54.61	−2.48	10008262	57.85%

Source: Bespoke Investment Group

HEDGE FUND EXPOSURE

Many consider hedge funds the "smart money," offering compensation that draws the best and the brightest. One part of the hedge fund world is in managed future contracts. Rather than picking individual stocks—buying Ford while shorting General Motors, for example—managed futures funds make directional bets on the market. As a group, they tend to follow trends. As a market goes up, for example, they will generally increase their exposure in a bet that the trend will continue. At extremes, though, they are fully committed and are at risk of the market moving against them, with little investor tolerance for loss at these maximum position points.

FIGURE 4.7 shows hedge fund exposure as calculated by Carpenter Analytical Services (CarpenterAnalytix.com). Note that hedge

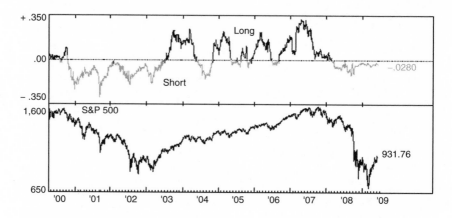

Figure 4.7   CTA hedge funds equity exposure, March 31, 2000 through June 3, 2009

Source: CarpenterAnalytix.com

funds were net short throughout the 2000 to 2002 bear market; they were generally on the correct side of the market because the long-term trend they were riding was a bearish one. Also note that they were the least short, during that timeframe, at the height of the bear market rallies and most short at the troughs.

In general, these funds aggressively follow trends and do well when a trend gets underway. However, these funds can grow overconfident once a trend becomes established. At these times of maximum exposure, the trend may be nearing its end.

RESOURCES

For a Bloomberg.com chart showing margin debt, Google "Bloomberg margdebt."

Carpenter Analytix has a variety of proprietary market indicators at www.carpenteranalytix.com. The Web site includes weekly market comments by the proprietor, Robin L. Carpenter.

Richard Bookstaber, author of *A Demon of Our Own Design*, occasionally posts on his blog (http://rick.bookstaber.com) his take on hedge fund activity in the markets.

Too Far, Too Fast

Whenever you find yourself on the side of the majority, it's time to pause and reflect.

—MARK TWAIN

STOCKS DON'T TRAVEL in a straight line. A bull market has pullbacks as owners doubt value and sell, which sometimes begets more selling. By the same token, bear markets have short-term rallies. This chapter will look· at a variety of measurements that suggest how "oversold" or "overbought" a market has become. A long-term investor might use these to better model buying and selling points. A shorter-term trader can catch a good portion of the rides up and back down, as investor spirits rise and fall.

Percent of Stocks above the 10-, 40-, 50- and 200-Day Moving Averages

Good decisions and good luck increase a firm's value over time, while poor decisions and bad luck do the opposite. Absent an extraordinary event, however, a company's true value doesn't change much from day to day. But its stock price may, underlining the sometimes-capricious nature of stock prices, and the importance of individual research and understanding. Much of the time, the market is approximately right. Sometimes, however, it gets carried away.

Many professionals view the 200-day moving average as a good proxy for the markets' longer-term view of a company's valuation. The Nasdaq Composite Index contains nearly three thousand stocks, representing a wide variety of companies. In a flat, range-bound market, about half these companies should trade above their 200-day moving averages. However, in a general bull market, more

Figure 5.1   Percent of Nasdaq stocks above their 200-day moving averages

Source: Chart courtesy of StockCharts.com (http://stockcharts.com)

firms gain perceived value and trade above their respective 200-day moving averages. The same is true of a general bear market, in which more firms lose perceived value and trade below their respective 200-day moving averages. An investor can gain clues about market direction by noticing the times that a majority of stocks are trading above or below this number.

FIGURE 5.1 shows the percentage of Nasdaq stocks trading above their 200-day moving average from 2002 through 2008.

Low readings generally marked periods of sharp sell-offs. In broad terms, these extremely low readings marked better times to buy than to sell. In many cases, the market digested whatever bad news was present and then rebounded somewhat.

High readings took longer to form and generally lasted longer than low readings. (Fear dissipates, but greed tends to linger.) In general, those periods marked good times for long-term investors to sell stock, raising cash to deploy during the next market sell-off.

The stock market had generally horrific years from March 2000 to March 2003. In the early months of 2003, the 200-day moving average price for most stocks had declined to a relatively low level. A combination of attractive valuations, the successful early days of the second Iraq War, and other bullish factors pushed the stock market to a sharp, sustained rally. Most stocks passed their 200-day moving averages. But the 200-day moving average takes up nearly ten months—around 80 percent of the market's two hundred and fifty trading days—so a high, sustained reading over one month did not necessarily indicate that the market was set for a sell-off.

This measure of stock market strength tends to peak ahead of price. Recall the discussion in Chapter 2 of Lowry's research into the "topping" nature of aging bull markets. The data suggested caution when averages continued to post new highs while the number of stocks participating declined, meaning that a few strong stocks were pulling the averages higher. In market terms, "breadth" was poor.

Throughout the bull market from 2003 into 2007, about 70 percent of stocks traded above their 200-day moving averages at each new market high. At the new high in October 2007, however, not even 50 percent of stocks were above their long-term averages. Apple (up 120 percent on the year, to $190) and Google (up 52 percent on the year, to $710) pulled the index higher, but stocks such as F5 Networks (down 10 percent) and Sears (down 23 percent) lagged. Apple and Google were terrific stocks to own at the time, but even the strongest lead dog needs help pulling the sled.

This analysis of current levels, in relation to recent readings, and the presence of sharp changes extends to studying other moving-average time frames.

SHORT-TERM SWINGS: THE 10-DAY MOVING AVERAGE

FIGURE 5.2 shows the percentage of Nasdaq stocks above their 10-day moving average during 2008. Most of the time, 20 to 80 percent of companies trade above their 10-day averages, as the market naturally fluctuates. The outlying points, the exceptions, are the most interesting. Spikes above 80 percent tended to coincide with short-term tops; quick drops below 20 percent coincided with bottoms.

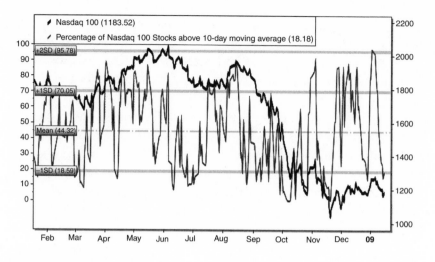

Figure 5.2   Percent of Nasdaq 100 stocks above their 10-day moving averages

Source: IndexIndicators.com

In an early 2007 study, Lowry's looked at eighteen cases since 1990 in which 10 percent or less of stocks traded below their 10-day moving average. They found that

- The market was up an average 2.98 percent in the next two weeks in fourteen of the eighteen instances.
- The market was up an average 8.9 percent in the next three months in seventeen of the eighteen examples.
- The market was up 20.1 percent in the next twelve months in seventeen of the eighteen examples.

These indicators are good reference points, but not hard-and-fast trading indicators. Conditions change over time, and the past is not always a prologue to the future.

It's important to remember, too, that short-term indicators tend to behave differently in bull and bear markets. In a bull market environment—one in which more than 60 percent of stocks are trading above their 200-day moving averages—there is more resilience and a higher chance of a strong snap-back rally when a 10-day reading that's below 20 percent signals a temporary downturn.

In a general bear market, by contrast, traders often see market strength as an opportunity to sell stocks. A deeply oversold market, with a 10-day reading of less than 20 percent, can feed on itself for a while in a bear market.

WORDEN T2108

Traders who use the TeleChart chart package (www.worden.com) can create their own templates or follow a wide choice of market metrics. One favorite is simply known as T2108. "What is T2108 doing" is shorthand among users for "how overbought or oversold is the market?" T2108 simply charts the percentage of stocks trading above their 40-day moving averages.

TeleChart users find this chart very useful in spotting oversold and overbought conditions, and many are devoted to its particular time frame. The 50-day moving average is more widely cited, and is typically analyzed as the average that falls between the 10-day and 200-day averages.

THE 50-DAY MOVING AVERAGE

FIGURE 5.3 shows the percentage of Nasdaq stocks trading above their 50-day moving averages from 2002 to 2008. Sharp declines to below 20 percent suggest that deeply oversold conditions are ripe for a bounce; a gradual decline suggests steady, constant selling of an unknown duration. Sustained multiweek readings of 70 percent suggest an unsustainable level of buying pressure. At the very least, traders should prepare for sideways trading as the market finds a new equilibrium. In many cases, a market pauses before resuming a longer-term rise or fall.

It's interesting to examine the period in which the market digested losses from the 2000–2002 bear market. In July 2002, only 6.7 percent of stocks traded above their 50-day averages. The market rallied substantially before falling back to a new low in early October, though with a higher 15 percent of stocks trading above their 50-day averages. The market rallied again before retesting the lows in March 2003, this time with 25 percent of stock trading below their 50-day averages. Fewer and fewer individual stocks remained below their near-term averages, suggesting some stocks enjoyed strengthening positions. This situation is also reflected in the 200-day chart (Figure 5.1).

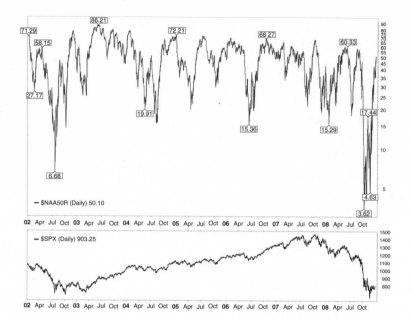

Figure 5.3 Percent of Nasdaq stocks above their 50-day moving average

Source: Chart courtesy of StockCharts.com (http://stockcharts.com)

COMBINING SHORT- AND LONG-TERM MOVING AVERAGES

Each moving average can yield its own insight. Another analytical approach is to combine two moving averages, an approach that helps incorporate the fact that indicator efficacy can differ in different market conditions. **FIGURE 5.4** shows the ratio of Nasdaq stocks above their 50-day moving averages to stocks above their 200-day moving averages. (See the averages that created these ratios above, in Figure 5.1 and Figure 5.3.)

In June 2006, for instance, prices were rising and the Federal Reserve was considering an interest-rate hike under the new leadership of Chairman Ben Bernanke. Market participants were unsure about how Bernanke would proceed. The percentage of stocks above their 50-day averages fell hard, while the 200-day number held up. This suggested an oversold condition within an ongoing bull market. The S&P 500 moved from roughly 1250 to 1350 as the ratio strengthened, then peaked in late September. The market continued to gain ground steadily until the bull market found its next oversold condition in March 2007.

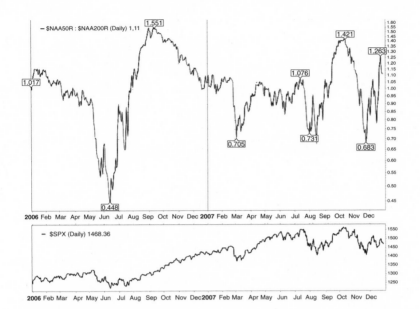

Figure 5.4 Ratio of Nasdaq stocks above 50-day moving average to 200-day moving average

Source: Chart courtesy of StockCharts.com (http://stockcharts.com)

SECTOR STRENGTH 50-DAY MOVING AVERAGES

Traders can enhance their study of overall market strength or weakness by considering which sectors contribute most to market conditions. Bespoke Investment Group offers a variety of market indicators, including an analysis by sector of the percentage of stocks trading above their 50-day moving averages. **FIGURE 5.5a** shows a twelve-month chart for the S&P 500, and **FIGURES 5.5b-f** show its ten major sectors for June 2007 through June 2008.

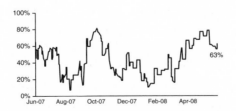

Figure 5.5a S&P 500 stocks above their 50-day moving average

Source: Bespoke Investment Group

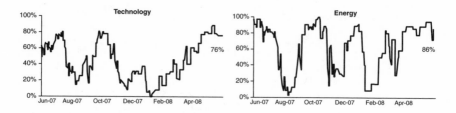

Figure 5.5b   Technology and energy stocks above their 50-day moving average

Source: Bespoke Investment Group

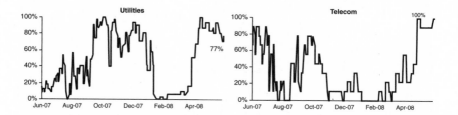

Figure 5.5c   Utilities and telecom stocks above their 50-day moving average

Source: Bespoke Investment Group

In June 2008, 63 percent of S&P 500 stocks were trading above their 50-day moving averages, an ordinary state of affairs. The sector scans, however, show that the technology (76 percent), energy (86 percent), utilities (77 percent), and telecom (100 percent) led the market. Momentum-based traders could have considered these sectors, as they showed the most sustained buying interest. Contratrend traders looking for snap-back rallies from deeply oversold conditions, as well as longer-term investors looking for buying opportunities among oversold stocks, were likely disappointed. With the financial sector (42 percent) as the weakest area, the market showed no obvious signs of distress.

Investors might also use these charts to take intermediate-term positions in sectors that the data suggests are in longer-term bull or bear markets. For instance, a trader convinced of a secular energy bull market could use the 50-day chart in Figure 5.5b to buy at the dips (times when stocks above their 50-day averages was less than

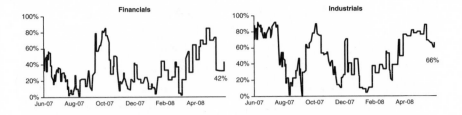

Figure 5.5d   Financial and industrial stocks above their 50-day moving average

Source: Bespoke Investment Group

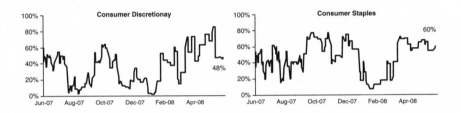

Figure 5.5e   Consumer discretionary and consumer staples stocks above their 50-day moving average

Source: Bespoke Investment Group

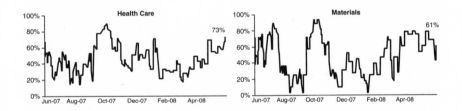

Figure 5.5f   Health-care and materials stocks above their 50-day moving average

Source: Bespoke Investment Group

15 percent) and to lighten up on the rallies (times when the same measure of 50-day averages was more than 85 percent). Investors might short a declining sector on the rallies and cover the position on a subsequent decline, as some investors did with financial sector stocks in 2008.

DISTANCE FROM 200-DAY MOVING AVERAGE

"Stocks will fluctuate," as J. P. Morgan said, and there are times when they fluctuate more than usual. **FIGURE 5.6** shows the price of crude oil from 1991 through 2008 in a logarithmic scale, to show relative price changes. For instance, the move in 1999 from roughly $12 to $25 per barrel was a greater percentage change than the move from $60 to $90 per barrel in 2007.

With oil at $50 a barrel and global demand running at nearly 85 million barrels per day, the oil market is worth nearly $1.5 trillion annually. Even so, it can still exhibit strong short-term price changes. The chart shows several times that the price strayed more than 20 percent from its 200-day average. A nine-year bull market included significant rallies and declines. Shorter-term traders who were aware of these large deviations from the mean found positioning opportunities. Longer-term investors could either adjust their positions or mentally prepare for a coming pause or reversal.

Figure 5.6   West Texas Intermediate crude oil prices from 1991 to 2008

Source: Chart courtesy of StockCharts.com (http://stockcharts.com)

It's more difficult to analyze individual stocks in this way. The smaller the asset in question, the greater the chance that the price will meaningfully deviate from its long-term average, often because of a specific event or a news item.

It can be misleadingly simple to see a long-term chart and decide what the market will do next on that alone. It's harder, however, to be right. An investor might have bet against oil in early 2000, for instance, because the price had stretched by 20 percent over its long-term average. That bet would have paid off, but only if the trader held the position for two years. Crude spiked to more than $37 in the interim, creating a 40 percent loss on a hypothetical short position. A trader might have found that loss difficult to carry, particularly if it were a large portfolio position.

New High/New Low Index

Traders can also look at price extremes by watching the number of stocks hitting 52-week highs and lows. Momentum-based investors and traders may view a strong "new high" reading as a bullish signal, characterizing a market in which participants are inclined toward excitement about firms' growth prospects and willing to pay increasingly higher prices for promises of future profits.

The same data can signal a generally favorable economic climate of rising corporate profits. For a momentum investor, a strong new high can signal that a long bear market is ending, and a substantial bull market is ready to take its place.

FIGURE 5.7 shows the 10-day new high/low ratio from 1999 thru 2008 for Nasdaq. Notice the sustained high reading in early 2003, when the market began to come out of a three-year sell-off. These repeated days of broad participation signaled tremendous buying pressure. A momentum investor, seeing this as a signal that the market had shifted from a headwind to a tailwind, might scan the new 52-week high list for the stocks that participated most in the rallies, then research which of those companies had the most promising growth profiles.

The fall of 2002 saw repeated downward spikes in new highs and new lows, as companies in general continued to report disappointing earnings, and disillusioned investors continued to abandon the market. A value-based investor could have looked at the new-low list as a source for companies beaten up in the broad market sell-off, then look to purchase their stocks at bargain prices.

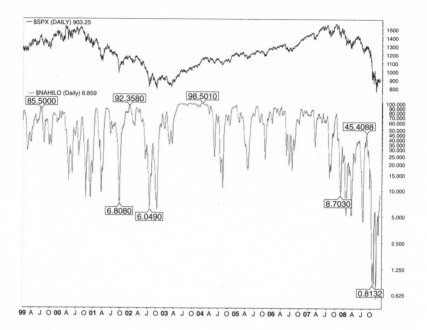

Figure 5.7 The 10-day average of the percent of Nasdaq stocks hitting 52-week highs

Buying and selling pressures change over the course of time. It is natural to see a very high reading on the new high list if the market has been selling off for months, as it eventually becomes easier for stocks to hit a new 52-week high. Traders are most interested in divergence, when market averages hit new highs or lows, while many stocks do not. Though the market may continue its trajectory, the data suggests that fewer and fewer stocks are pulling it in that direction. The tide is turning.

One can see this dynamic in 2002, which showed lower ratios as the market sold off. Every new market low was accompanied by a lesser number of companies making new 52-week lows. The market was stabilizing.

The data can also suggest that the market will continue its course. In 2008's October sell-off, fewer than 1 percent of stocks hit a 52-week high. In 2002's earlier, brutal bear market, more than 6 percent of stocks hit new highs. The 2008 sell-off was unusually broad, with few stocks showing strength.

Charts are a good way to follow this data, but an investor might also gain insight from *Barron's* weekly list of stocks making new highs and lows, or from the stock tables put out by *Investor's Business Daily*. It's obvious when one side is overwhelming the other—hundreds of new highs with just a handful of new lows, for instance. Again, a momentum investor could use the new high list to find stocks that are drawing sustained buying interest, especially when the market is healthy and new highs greatly outnumber new lows. Deep value investors can also use the list, in this case to find stocks that the market particularly disdains—an especially interesting exercise when the entire market is down.

The Arms Index—Adding Volume to the Equation

One central trading tenet is that, without substantial volume, market moves don't mean much. Light price moves don't generally reflect what bigger moneymakers are thinking or doing, though they do show a signal on the advance-decline line.

In 1967, market technician Richard Arms developed an index analyzing the relationship between advancing and declining issues and their respective volume. The Arms Index is also widely known as the TRIN, which stands for TRading INdex.

The TRIN is calculated using the following formula:

(Number of Advancing Issues/Number of Declining Issues)/
(Advancing Volume/Declining Volume),

where "advancing volume" is the cumulative volume of the stocks up on the day.

In a balanced market, the number of advancing and declining issues is roughly the same and the volume on both sides is approximately equal, giving an Arms value of one. Because the Arms Index incorporates price movement and volume, it can act as a useful measure of market supply and demand over different time frames.

Many consider the market overbought when the 10-day moving average declines to below 0.8, and oversold when it moves past 1.2. Richard Arms has written extensively and his original book, *The Arms Index (TRIN)* (McGraw-Hill, 1989), more fully illustrates how he uses this indicator.

FIGURE 5.8 shows the 10-day moving average on the TRIN during 2007. Spikes above 1.2 signaled good intermediate buying points, as the price moves and accompanying volume marked

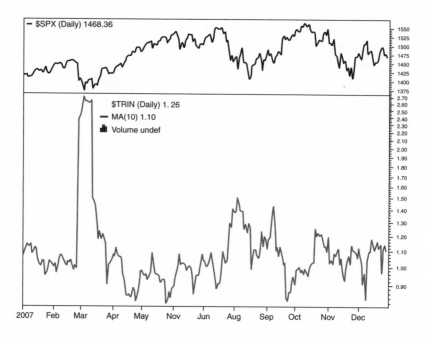

Figure 5.8   The 10-day TRIN average during 2007

Source: Chart courtesy of StockCharts.com (http://stockcharts.com)

capitulation-level selling. Those few times the level neared 0.8 may have helped investors determine when buying pressure was reaching a climax.

RESOURCES

The Web site www.indexindicators.com offers a wide variety of market indicators without charge for a wide array of global markets. The chart included in this chapter of the percent of stocks above their 10-day moving averages can be found under the Breadth Indicators tab.

Find market commentary and statistics from Bespoke Investment Group at www.bespokeinvest.typepad.com. It comments periodically on the sector breakdown of stocks trading above their 50-day moving averages.

Barron's publishes a list of the weekly highs and lows in the weekly "Market Labs" section. The Saturday version of *Investor's Business Daily* (*IBD*) also highlights stock movements on a weekly basis. Many momentum-based traders find *IBD* very useful in profiling high-growth stocks and specifically provide indicators showing improvement in company fundamentals and institutional interest/accumulation.

Relative Value

Though the stock market functions as a voting machine in the short run, it acts as a weighing machine in the long run.

—BENJAMIN GRAHAM

The four most expensive words in the English language are, "This time it's different."

—SIR JOHN TEMPLETON

MANY MODELS ATTEMPT to characterize whether the current market is cheap or dear. They incorporate a variety of economic indicators, including aggregate money flows (such as M2), inflation (CPI), expected inflation, and the unemployment rate. They consider stock market measures such as price to earnings ratio (P/E), earnings momentum, or book value. Some look at currency rates, commodity prices, or even sun spot activity. The list goes on and on.

Today's cheap computer power, accessible historical data, and robust software packages offer nonprogrammers statistical modeling that was previously available only to the most sophisticated professional traders. But it's not easy to forecast the future. Investors often react in similar ways over time, but the patterns can shift in seemingly random ways, frustrating those who assume that the future will exactly mirror the past. The world's events are correlated in ways that are easy to see in retrospect, but nearly impossible to anticipate consistently.

It is still difficult, but much more likely, to come to an approximately accurate future prediction through a model of the past. Many investors have said that they would rather be approximately right than exactly wrong. The models here help investors accomplish that goal.

I don't believe in mathematics.

—ALBERT EINSTEIN

The Fed Model

The granddaddy of stock models is elegantly simple, widely known, and heavily criticized as fundamentally flawed.

A July 1997 paper written by three Federal Reserve employees contained an investigation of the relationship between earnings yield and Treasury yield; it was then the latest in a long line of research on the relationship between stocks and bonds. Dr. Edward Yardeni, currently president of Yardeni Research, then a market strategist at Prudential Securities, found the paper of interest, studied the concept, and dubbed it the "Fed model" when he extended it to the market as a forecasting tool. (The Federal Reserve, ironically, doesn't endorse the method or use it in their policy decisions, but the name stuck anyway.)

The Fed model is centered on the premise that the bond market is the largest alternative to the stock market. If the bonds yield more than equities, investors are better off buying bonds. The model defines equity yield as earnings per share divided by current stock price. For instance, if IBM is expected to earn $6 per share next year and its stock price is $100, then its forward earnings yield is 6 percent.

The model's key assumption is that the 10-year Treasury note yield should be similar to the S&P 500 forward earnings yield. If the yields are not similar, the Fed model suggests that traders sell the lower-yielding instrument and buy the higher-yielding alternative.

FIGURE 6.1 shows the market's expected return based on the Fed model. According to that model, the S&P 500 was tremendously overvalued relative to Treasury bonds in December 1999. Only an S&P 500 decrease, a Treasury bond rally, or a combination of both could bring this basic relationship back in balance. In 2000, the 10-year bond substantially rallied, with the rate going from 6.4 percent to 5.0 percent as the S&P 500 declined 9.1 percent ('old' bonds

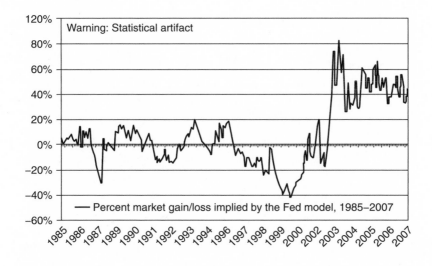

Figure 6.1 Fed model forecasted equity moves from 1985 through 2007

Source: Hussman Funds

paying higher interest are worth more when 'new' bonds are issued with lower interest payments).

By the middle of 2002, the model again suggested that the market was an attractive alternative to benchmark Treasury bonds.

The Fed model's strength is in its simplicity. It has only two inputs, is easy to understand, and compares two of the most basic investment options—stocks or bonds?—an investor faces.

Simplicity is also the Fed model's weakness. *It has only two inputs.* The model doesn't factor in the current or projected inflation that can erode bond value, nor note the partial inflation protection that equities can offer. (Bond terms don't change, but business owners can raise prices.) It doesn't factor in international money flows, which tend to concentrate their buying in Treasuries. (When China ran a huge trade surplus, the money found its way to Treasuries, depressing yield). It also uses estimated earnings and, as examined in Chapter 8, those estimates are suspect at best. Finally, as market commentator and money manager John Hussman has researched, the Fed model was a poor predictor when the data is extrapolated to decades before 1985. It may be intuitively enticing, but the Fed model does not pass deeper scrutiny.

The Alternative: BBB Corporate Bonds

Portfolio manager and market commentator David Merkel puts his own spin on the Fed model on his blog (www.alephblog.com). Instead of comparing equities to Treasury bonds, however, he uses corporate bonds, which he thinks are a better proxy for modeling the relative value of stocks. This model, he believes, comes closer to matching the true cost of owning either bonds or equities.

The differences between stocks and bonds, Merkel points out, are in risk and growth. Bondholders enjoy regular coupon payments when things go well, and retain ownership of the reorganized firm if the business files for bankruptcy. A bond offers less risk than an equity investment—but it doesn't offer a chance to participate in business growth.

Equity holders may receive dividends; more important, they participate in a firm's growth. (Earnings growth has averaged 6.7 percent annually over the past fifty-five years, a rate that this model assumes will continue.) If the firm fails, however, they're typically left with nothing.

To compensate for taking extra risk, a trader who buys S&P 500 equities should demand a forward earnings yield of 2.5 percent to 3 percent more than the prevailing BBB bond rate, an extra required return known as the risk premium. If that's not available, an investor is better off buying corporate bonds instead.

To review the model's inputs:

1. A bondholder receives the BBB corporate rate.
2. An equity holder must beat the BBB rate by 2.5 percent to 3.0 percent (a middle ground of 2.8 percent in this calculation) to compensate for the higher risk, but enjoys a 6.7 percent average earnings growth rate.

BBB Corporate Rate
= S&P Earnings Yield − 2.8 Percent Risk Premium
  + 6.7 Percent Earnings Growth

Buy stocks if the S&P earnings yield is greater than the BBB rate minus 3.9 percent. Otherwise, buy bonds.

A BBB bond yield of 8.9 percent would support an S&P 500 trading at a price/earnings ratio of 20, or an earnings yield of

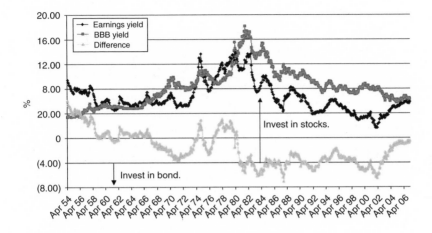

Figure 6.2   Comparing earnings yield to BBB bond yield

Source: alephblog.com

5 percent. **FIGURE 6.2** tracks the equity earnings yield for S&P 500 stocks as a group versus the BBB bond yield, between April 1954 and April 2006.

For much of the time between 1981 and 2003, the data suggests that an investor would have been better off in the bond market than in equities. A bondholder would have missed the chance to boast about the Ciena Corporation (networks) when it seemingly went up by nearly 10 percent a day in 1999, but the bond investor probably slept better at night. From 1954 to 1981, by contrast, stocks would have been the better investment.

Dividend Yield

Dividend yield can also be predictive, as two posts on the Capital Spectator blog (www.capitalspectator.com) suggest. Many academic studies say that relative dividend yield is important, and that low dividend yields point to subpar future returns (and vice versa). Capital Spectator agrees, but adds that this predictive capability has varied over the past one hundred and fifty years.

FIGURE 6.3 shows the ebb and flow of the relevance of dividends to future stock performance. R-squared is a statistical measurement for the correlation between two variables. An R-squared of 1.0 means perfect correlation: variables move in lockstep. An R-squared of

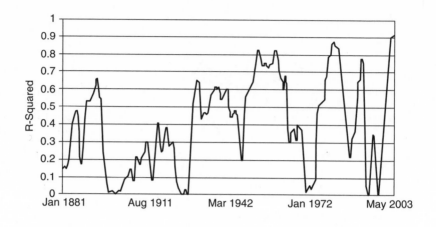

Figure 6.3   Predictive value of dividend yield, 1880–2003

Source: Robert Shiller

0 means absolutely no correlation. The chart shows that sometimes dividends are good predictors of future five-year returns. Sometimes they are not. The Capital Spectator says:

1. Always be skeptical about methods of achieving certain market profits. As this graph shows, even intellectually sound ideas move in and out of favor through the sweep of time.
2. A good indicator should factor in the larger economic and financial contexts. Looking at absolute dividend yield without considering interest rates is shortsighted, as shown here.
3. As an indicator, dividend yield, like most market metrics, works better when it reaches extremes relative to recent history. Capital Spectator suggests looking at relative highs and lows relative to the last twenty years, not the last one hundred and fifty years.

Building a Better Mousetrap: Proprietary Models

From investment banks to boutique shops, many advisory services use all sorts of data to forecast the stock market. They devote a tremendous amount of brainpower to looking at historical relationships. BCA (Bank Credit Analyst) Research serves institutional investors, and has been developing models for more than fifty years. BCA releases a periodic snapshot of its views and various indicators to the public at www.bcaresearch.com.

VALUE LINE

Most investors know Value Line as the research service that sends subscribers one-page research reports, individually covering more than seventeen hundred stocks. Analysts include their expectations for the next three to five years of a stock's performance, given the company's financial position and growth prospects, in the upper left section of every stock report. Each week, Value Line publishes the average of these expected returns for all the stocks they cover. (Look for the "Estimated Median Price Appreciation Potential," directly under the table of contents.) Academics have studied this number, calling it the "Value Line median appreciation potential," or VLMAP.

Daniel Seiver, an economist who edits an investment newsletter called the *PAD System Report*, and the late Peter Bernstein, a prolific author who edited an institutional investor newsletter called *Economics & Portfolio Strategy*, are responsible for much of the research on the VLMAP. As a market signal, Seiver uses a reading of 100 percent or more as a buy signal. A reading of 100 percent argues that Value Line stocks are expected to double in value in the next three to five years. When stocks are trading at 50 percent or less of the level Value Line analysts collectively believe it will achieve in three to five years, the market is oversold and it's time to buy. A reading of 50 percent or more serves as a sell signal. In Seiver's view, this number indicates that the market is just not priced at a level that suggests the potential rewards of owning stock outweighs the risk.

Value Line also comments on its outlook for the market, indicating whether it sees a global "buy" or "sell." Value Line doesn't publicize the metrics it considers, but it likely looks at the metrics Seiver and Bernstein describe.

MARKET COMMENTATORS

John Hussman and Jeremy Grantham are two of the better-known market commentators who use researched market history to help guide their decisions. Hussman runs the Hussman Funds and posts weekly commentary at www.hussmanfunds.com. Grantham is chairman of the board at Grantham Mayo Van Otterloo. He periodically reveals his seven-year forecast of expected returns among asset classes at www.gmo.com. Both offer written outlooks giving insight into how these portfolio managers and students of market history view the current investment climate.

SECTOR WEIGHTINGS

Charles Henry Dow, who founded the *Wall Street Journal* (then called the *Customers' Afternoon Letter*), composed the first stock index. In the early days of the newspaper, Dow focused on Wall Street, hoping it would prove a way to stand apart from the crowd of other dailies. Dow thought the best way to capture daily market movements was to create one number reflecting the net change of the largest stocks, thereby representing a cross section of the U.S. economy. On May 26, 1896, Dow introduced his index of twelve companies, which had an initial value of 40.94. Being an immodest sort, he dubbed it the Dow Jones Industrial Average (DJIA). (Edward Davis Jones was a fellow founding reporter but had nothing to do with devising the index for which he is famous.) Over time, the index came to include thirty companies, and became the public's eye on the market.

This index has two structural issues. The first is that it is equal-weighted. A $1 change in any stock has an equal impact on the index reading, no matter the firm's market capitalization or the percentage change a price move represents. If IBM moves up $1 to $101 (a 1 percent change), this affects the index reading as much as Pfizer's move from $20 to $21 (a 5 percent change). Second, the U.S. economy has gained both size and complexity since 1896. Thirty stocks can represent the vast American market, but more stocks would do a better job.

Standard and Poor's recognized these limitations and introduced the S&P 500 on March 4, 1957. This index is market capitalization-weighted, so a 1 percent change in Exxon Mobil, which has a market capitalization of approximately $400 billion, gets ten times the weight of Medtronic, with a market capitalization of around $40 billion. It better reflects the net change in the underlying value of U.S. business. The five hundred companies included in the index allow Standard and Poor's to better match the index to how the U.S. economy is currently functioning and valued.

The U.S. economy evolves over generations, but the basics don't change much from year to year. People have a baseline need for utilities, such as water and electricity, and often work under government price constraints. It would be surprising to see spikes in the relative importance (and valuation) of utility companies. The same can be said for the broad industries that provide basic goods, including technology, finance, and consumer staples.

It can be useful to spot times that a basic industry or sector is over- or underrepresented in the S&P 500, as compared to its long-term average. Any substantial deviation suggests a fundamental and permanent shift in that industry's influence, or suggests that the market is giving more or less respect than a given industry deserves.

FIGURE 6.4 shows the historical sector weightings of the S&P 500 from 1990 through 2008. Some observable trends seem obvious in hindsight, but at the time were heralded as the dawn of a new era.

Technology, for instance, went from a weighting of 5.1 percent in 1992 (when the sector bellwether at the time, IBM, traded at $12) to 17.7 percent in 1998 (when IBM stood at $90 and many thought the sector was overvalued) to a peak 29.2 percent in the tech glory days of 1999. The sector sold off to a relatively consistent 16 percent weighting after 2003. The following are a few lessons:

- Sometimes there *are* profound shifts in the makeup of the economy, and good reasons for a sector to take up a larger portion of the S&P 500.
- At the same time, markets can and do get carried away. It was hard for many commentators in 1999 to believe that technology could really make up thirty percent of the U.S. economy. Ultimately, shareholders decided that they didn't believe it either, as the pace of technology profit growth subsided.
- The energy sector was overweighted and the consumer discretionary sector was underweighted, but weightings were otherwise roughly in line during 2007. Perhaps as a result, all sectors participated in roughly equal proportions in the 2008 sell-off.

WANTS VERSUS NEEDS

Which is doing better in the stock market: Procter & Gamble's toothpaste, or Best Buy's flat-screen televisions? The answer gives insight into both the state of the economy and market money flow.

Sector	1990	1992	1994	1996	1997	1998	1999	2000	2001	2002	2003	2004	2006	2007	7/15	9/19	Current
Financials	7.5	10.6	10.7	15.0	17.2	15.4	13.0	17.3	17.8	20.5	20.7	20.6	22.3	17.6	12.9	16.4	16.0
Technology	6.3	5.1	8.6	12.4	12.3	17.7	29.2	21.2	17.6	14.3	17.7	16.1	15.1	16.7	16.7	15.7	15.9
Health Care	10.4	9.9	9.2	10.4	11.3	12.3	9.3	14.4	14.4	14.9	13.3	12.7	12.0	12.0	12.9	12.5	13.7
Energy	13.4	9.7	10.0	9.2	8.4	6.3	5.6	6.6	6.3	6.0	5.8	7.2	9.8	12.9	15.3	13.6	12.8
Consumer Staples	14.0	14.5	13.2	12.7	12.3	11.1	7.2	8.1	8.2	9.5	11.0	10.5	9.3	10.2	11.6	11.7	12.4
Industrials	13.6	13.3	13.0	12.7	11.7	10.1	9.9	10.6	11.3	11.5	10.9	11.8	10.8	11.5	11.2	11.2	11.0
Consumer Discretionary	12.8	15.8	14.9	11.7	12.1	12.5	12.7	10.3	13.1	13.4	11.3	11.9	10.6	8.5	8.1	8.7	8.0
Utilities	6.2	5.6	4.8	3.7	3.3	3.0	2.2	3.8	3.1	2.9	2.8	2.9	3.6	3.6	4.1	3.5	3.6
Materials	7.2	6.9	7.1	5.8	4.5	3.1	3.0	2.3	2.6	2.8	3.0	3.1	3.0	3.3	3.9	3.7	3.3
Telecom	8.7	8.5	8.6	6.5	6.9	8.4	7.9	5.5	5.5	4.2	3.5	3.3	3.5	3.6	3.4	3.1	3.3

Figure 6.4 Historical sector weightings

Source: Bespoke Investment Group

In broad terms, firms in the consumer staples sector provide basic necessities. Companies such as Costco, Procter & Gamble, and Clorox are typical of this group. Their earnings are less vulnerable to the economic cycle. The Consumer Staples Select SPDR ETF (XLP) tracks this group.

Stocks in the consumer discretionary sector, on the other hand, represent firms providing the little luxuries people enjoy, but don't *have* to have. Companies such as Starbucks, Wynn Resorts, and Electronic Arts (video games) characterize this group. Firms in this category often have lumpier income streams than do consumer staples companies, and show earnings growth mainly during strong economies. The Consumer Discretionary SPDR ETF (XLY) tracks the performance of these companies. Comparing how these two groups are doing can give insight into the state of the economy and the risk tolerance of the market at large.

FIGURE 6.5 shows the ratio of XLY (discretionary sector) to XLP (staples sector) on a weekly basis from 2001 through 2008. Notice that

1) When the economic outlook appears poor and investors want a maximum defensive posture, they tend to sell discretionary stocks and buy staples. They migrate to the companies offering the most stable and predictable revenue streams. Steep drops in the ratio suggest investors have become too cautious, and point toward a migration away from safer stocks. The four-week rate of change (ROC (4)) measures these extremes, which are circled on the chart.

2) Over a longer time frame, the data reveals investor risk tolerance and the broad economic outlook. When the longer-term ratio is trending down, investors see economic weakness ahead and move toward less cyclical assets. A longer trend up suggests an improving economy, with investors migrating toward companies with a higher growth profile. Graph trend lines show these moves.

TOBIN'S QUOTIENT RATIO

Instead of looking at earnings—past, present, and future —Tobin's quotient ratio (the Q) looks at the economy's collective productive assets, and at how highly the stock market values those assets. Nobel Prize-winning economist James Tobin developed this ratio in 1969.

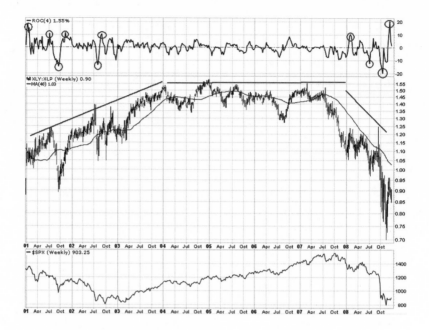

Figure 6.5   Consumer discretionary to consumer staples

Source: Chart courtesy of StockCharts.com (http://stockcharts.com)

It compares a company's valuation to its replacement value, using the following calculation:

Tobin's Q = (Equity Market Value + Liabilities Book Value)/
(Equity Book Value + Liabilities Book Value)

FIGURE 6.6 shows the Q ratio from 1952 through 2008.

If the ratio is above 1.0, the ratio implies that the market values companies at more than their replacement costs. The further the ratio moves above 1.0, the more sense it makes for entrepreneurs to build new businesses and take them public. Creating new competition should, over the long term, pressure current corporate margins and act as a general headwind for stocks.

A ratio below 1.0 suggests stocks are undervalued, because they are typically cheaper than the comparable cost of starting a new firm. A wealthy person would be better off buying stocks in the open market than trying to start new companies.

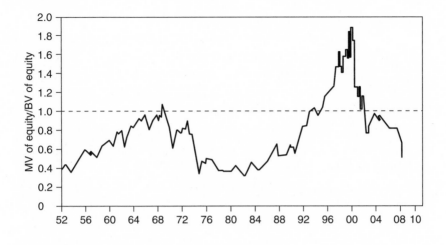

Figure 6.6   Ratio of equity value to book value

Source: PIMCO

In the late 1990s, many analysts pointed to Tobin's Q ratio as proof that the market's advance was unsustainable, because it had far eclipsed the value of the market's underlying hard assets. Others countered that the economy had changed since Tobin composed the ratio in 1969. Business value increasingly consisted of technical know-how; a firm's most enduring value was not in land and machinery but in patents and other specialized, hard-to-replicate knowledge. IBM's value, for instance, was not in its chip plant or office buildings, but in its enduring brand value, unmatched patent portfolio, and deep consulting relationships with *Fortune* 500 customers. Those economically vital assets have very little book value.

Notice that the chart in Figure 6.6 shows a long-term average for Tobin's Q that is well below 1.0. The reason, some argue, is that book value overstates the open-market replacement value of companies' assets.

Nonetheless, the Q is an enduring indicator because it doesn't estimate earnings or make other bets on the future. It simply reveals market value in terms of hard, productive assets.

SHILLER'S CAPE

Yale professor and market historian Robert Shiller argues that one year of watching either trailing twelve-month or forward expected twelve-month earnings is not long enough to correctly capture a firm's earnings profile. Measuring ten years of trailing earnings and comparing them to the current stock price, he says, is a better way to measure a company's earning power over a complete business cycle. This long-term, retrospective measure is called the cyclically adjusted price/earnings (CAPE) ratio.

The CAPE shows that the market can move away from its long-term earnings value, sometimes for long stretches. **FIGURE 6.7** shows the market's ratio since 1880 using the 10-year CAPE. The average CAPE ratio over the past one hundred and thirty years has been about 15. Prices may fluctuate around this basic valuation and have stretched far above *and* below it, but Shiller argues that the market eventually reverts to this *long*-term mean. This doesn't help a short-term trader, but a long-term investor can use CAPE to gain a sense of the market's current position relative to its long-term norm. Buying stocks at generally low CAPE levels argues for good returns over a long period of time.

According to this model, the market was overvalued from 1992 to the end of 2008. In 1910, 1929, and 1966, the CAPE went significantly above its trend line, but valuations did not come back to fair value and stay there. They overshot to the downside. This chart suggests that a new investor entering the market at the end of 2008 could expect long-term returns of 6 percent to 7 percent if past

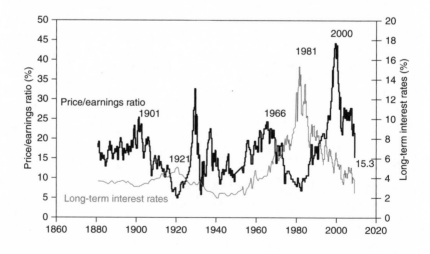

Figure 6.7   Shiller's CAPE ratio, 1860–2008

Source: Robert Shiller

market trends continued. The same investor, however, shouldn't be surprised to see the market go to a much lower valuation or move sideways while corporate earnings continued to grow.

The chart (Figure 6.7) suggests that the CAPE was in undervalued territory between the mid-1970s and the early 1980s, but moved into a better valuation as inflation quieted and price/earnings multiples expanded.

THE REALLY BIG PICTURE

Comparing the market value of all publicly traded companies to the country's total production output for the year gives another twenty-thousand-foot market view. Warren Buffett did this in a 1999 *Fortune* article, with writer Carol Loomis. (The duo revisited the topic in 2009.)

Buffett argued that, over the long run, it is impossible for the market to outgrow the economy. It can do so for periods of time in which corporations can increase profit margins, but is constrained in the end. In 1999, when the ratio peaked at 190 percent (stocks were valued at almost twice the country's gross national product), Buffett said he would be interested in buying if the ratio moved into a range between 70 and 80 percent, and indeed was buying in late 2008, when the ratio was near 75 percent. This ratio has been as low as 40 percent and has sometimes stayed there for years, as it did from roughly 1945 to 1955 and between 1975 and 1985.

"For me, the message is this: if the percentage relationship falls to the 70 percent or 80 percent area, buying stocks is likely to work well for you. If the ratio approaches 200 percent—as it did in 1999 and a part of 2000—you are playing with fire," Buffett noted in the 2009 *Fortune* article.

RESOURCES

David Merkel is a money manager and market commentator. His insights can be found on his Web site at www.alephblog.com.

Among independent research firms, BCA Research is one widely followed by institutional investors. BCA Research daily commentary on its research and conclusions is available on its Web site at www.bcaresearch.com.

Find market commentary and statistics from Bespoke Investment Group at www.bespokeinvest.typepad.com. The company comments periodically on the historical sector weightings of the S&P 500, among many other indicators.

Part II

Considering the Human Element

Not everything that can be counted counts, and not everything that counts can be counted.

—ALBERT EINSTEIN

IN THE FIRST PART OF THIS BOOK, we reviewed a wide variety of methods that examine and compare numerical market data. The results offer clues to the future direction of stocks, sectors, and markets. These are useful, worthwhile tools.

For all its usefulness, however, ratios and charts are not the only thing to consider when looking for ways to make better-informed investment decisions. Numbers, with their cold, hard logic, don't operate companies or deliver services. They can't model the inherent chaos of life, nor account for the surprisingly frequent accuracy of human gut feeling.

I got a taste of that accuracy shortly after my first management interview with the CEO of a small hardware chain. They had sustained ongoing operating losses, and investors were concerned that competition from The Home Depot and Lowe's were overwhelming them. But the chain was shifting to specialize in serving professional contractors, a niche management claimed was strong, and had land and buildings with a cost basis that went back decades. We felt the balance sheet undervalued this asset. One of their divisions made windows and was itself profitable. If they shut down all their stores, sold their land, and auctioned the window division to pay creditors, we estimated, their shares would still be worth more than the $5 current stock price. If management could better manage their business and show even meager profits, it was reasonable to expect a $10 to $12 valuation. It seemed like a good risk-to-reward scenario.

We met with the CFO and then the CEO. We asked our questions. They did their best to avoid direct answers. After the meeting, my boss asked me what I thought. I shrugged my shoulders—this was new to me. What did he think? "I need to take a shower, that guy was so slimy," he replied.

Strong competition and operating losses gave my boss a warning, but his visceral reaction to the CEO sealed his negative opinion of the company's future. And he was right. Eighteen months and a string of poor management decisions later, the company was bankrupt. It had rung up more debt and backed it with real estate, which turned out to be worth less than we thought.

Stockholders got nothing. Nada. Zilch. It is the one stock I've ridden to zero. After that, if I met with management and got the same, bad feeling, I got out of the position and didn't look back, no matter what the numbers said.

Reading a situation, listening to your instincts (and those of more experienced investors), and employing common sense don't show up in many data analyses, but all three can save an investor's financial hide. The second section of this book examines ways one might look at the market's human factor, and what clues one might derive from the results.

Chapter 7

Sentiment Surveys

When there is a boom and everyone is scrambling for common stocks, take all your stocks and sell them. Put the proceeds in the bank. No doubt, the stocks you sold will go higher. Pay no attention to this—just wait for the recession which will come sooner or later. When it gets bad enough to arouse the politicians to make speeches, take your money out of the bank and buy back the stocks. No doubt the stocks will go still lower. Again pay no attention. Wait for the next boom. Continue to repeat this operation as long as you live, and you'll have the pleasure of dying rich.

—FRED SCHWED JR., *Where Are the Customers' Yachts?:
or A Good Hard Look at Wall Street,* 1940

The most common cause of low prices is pessimism—some times pervasive, some times specific to a company or industry. We want to do business in such an environment, not because we like pessimism but because we like the prices it produces. It's optimism that is the enemy of the rational buyer.

—WARREN BUFFETT, in his 1990 annual
letter to shareholders

JUST AS POLITICIANS take straw polls to gauge public opinion, a variety of established surveys track how investors currently view the market. In revealing an opinion, investors also typically reveal their current market positioning. Investors bullish on the future, for instance, are likely already fully committed in stocks. They "talk their book" or believe according to how they're positioned.

This chapter's surveys examine investor outlooks in different ways, and can help a savvy reader know when to zig when many are zagging, as well as when it's better to go with the flow.

American Association of Individual Investors

The American Association of Individual Investors (AAII) is a non-profit organization founded in 1978; it exists to "assist individuals in becoming effective managers of their own assets through programs of education, information, and research." Since 1987, each week its one hundred and fifty thousand members can indicate (at www.aaii. com) whether they are bullish, bearish, or neutral on the stock market over the next six months.

Investors can use a sentiment survey such as this one as a reality check for their own market views, remembering that most people think in a linear fashion and extrapolate the past into the future. Take the example of a grinding bear market, which typically creates a gradual increase in the ranks of bearish investors. If an investor sees significant, underappreciated problems on the market's horizon, a mildly bearish survey reading may support the thesis that people recognize the outlines of the issues, but not the severity. They are bearish, but not bearish *enough*. If the survey echoed the investor's bearish sentiments, the poor outlook would more likely be reflected in stock prices.

FIGURE 7.1 shows the percent of AAII members with bullish six-month outlooks during 2007 and 2008. Instances where the reading went from a relatively high to low level in just a few weeks signaled significant investor concern. Consider December 2007, when 50 percent of members shared a bullish outlook; that number dropped to less than 20 percent in just a few weeks and formed a fifty-two-week low. At the time, the S&P 500 dropped from 1500 to nearly 1300, and investors thought the hard sell-off would continue. By the time the reading reached 50 percent in May, the S&P 500 had rebounded to over 1400.

AAII also polls members monthly regarding their current asset allocation between stocks, bonds, and cash. Typically, high cash levels correspond with highly bearish outlooks and sentiment readings. See current results for both surveys at www.aaii.com/research.

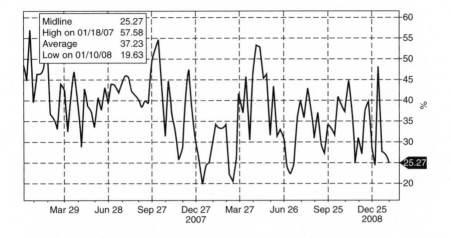

Midline	25.27
High on 01/18/07	57.58
Average	37.23
Low on 01/10/08	19.63

Mar 29   Jun 28   Sep 27   Dec 27   Mar 27   Jun 26   Sep 25   Dec 25
2007   2008

Figure 7.1   Percentage of AAII bulls, 2007–2008

Source: Bloomberg

Investors Intelligence

Investors Intelligence (II) is a survey of more than one hundred and thirty investment newsletters, conducted weekly by Chartcraft since 1963 through all sorts of markets. II is a subjective measurement of advice from financial newsletter writers. Newsletter writers have a natural bullish tendency—the product they're selling is generally geared towards stock ownership, and stocks have tended to rise over time. II deems a newsletter "neutral" if the writer is bullish in the long term but expects a short-term correction. Survey administrators call a reading "normal" when it measures 45 percent bullish, 35 percent bearish, and 20 percent neutral advice.

FIGURE 7.2 shows the difference between bullish and bearish advisers from 2006 through 2008. From a peak +40 percent bearish reading in October 2007, sentiment steadily deteriorated. Each successive rally met with a lower sentiment reading than before; each sell-off brought a new low.

Sharp drops in sentiment often marked tradable lows. Note the sharp drop in August 2007, when the sentiment reading dropped from +35 percent to +10 percent in a matter of two weeks. This turned out to reflect an oversold condition that reversed itself over the following two months.

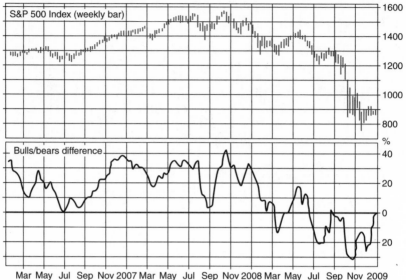

Figure 7.2 Percent difference between bullish and bearish advisers, 2006–2008

Source: InvestorsIntelligence.com

More information on the II survey and the company's other research can be found at www.investorsintelligence.com. Look for the periodic, delayed II Insight, a weekly report that includes a recent advisers' sentiment index and the editor's read of the current market. Services such as SentimenTrader and DecisionPoint offer charts based on this survey.

Market Vane

Every week, Market Vane surveys trading recommendations from the leading market advisers and commodity trading advisers (CTAs). They examine outlooks for all investable asset classes, including equities, precious metals, and agricultural products.

Market Vane collects advisers' letters, listens to hotlines, and calls major brokerage houses to hear recommendations in the various markets. The result is a measurement of the consensus among bullish advisers for each market. Market Vane argues that if enough advisers are bullish, money will flow into that market and prices will rise. **FIGURE 7.3**

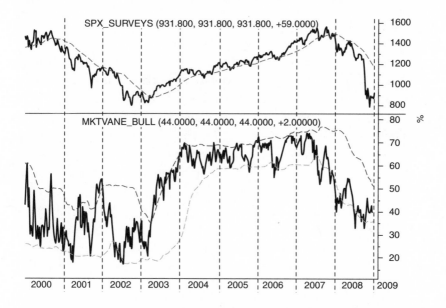

Figure 7.3   Percentage of bullish Market Vane advisers

Source: Market Vane

shows the Market Vane reading for the S&P 500 from 2000 through 2008.

As with the advisers' sentiment index in Figure 7.2, bullish totals got progressively lower *before* the market top in October 2007, because some advisers pulled their bullish calls at the correct time. Bear market lows in late 2002 also coincided with a less bearish reading, as a significant number of advisers told clients to increase their stock holdings at approximately the right time.

Those interested in sentiment readings for gold, wheat, oil, or other assets outside the main stock market should consider this resource. Find the weekly stock market consensus reading in *Barron's* Market Lab section.

Hulbert Newsletter Survey

Mark Hulbert is a senior writer for financial site MarketWatch.com and often writes about various sentiment indicators. Since 1980, he has tracked the advice and performance of more than one hundred and eighty newsletters, telling subscribers which advisers have track records that back their claims and which advisers to avoid.

Hulbert's deep database shows how short- and long-term investing advisers are currently directing their clients. He uses the short-term outlook to compile his Hulbert Stock Newsletter Sentiment Index (HSNSI). (For advisers with a longer-term horizon, Hulbert looks for writers with a sustained good record, independently verifying the performance that the newsletter writers claim.)

Then, he uses this indicator to find extreme readings and points of divergence. For instance, an increasing level of bullishness is the normal reaction to a rising market. If a strong market were met with a stable or declining level of adviser bullishness, that might indicate a lack of trust or buy-in for the advance, and (perversely) a greater chance the current bullish trend continues, because sidelined money can still be committed. As with other indicators, a sharp change in adviser outlook suggests an overreaction to current events and the possibility that the market will at least partially self-correct.

Find more information on Hulbert's service at www.marketwatch. com.

Merrill Lynch Fund Manager Survey

Every month, Merrill Lynch (now part of Bank of America) surveys almost two hundred money managers from around the world about their economic and market outlooks. Merrill uses this data to create various ratios the company shares with clients, and also releases a monthly report that outlines survey findings. (Find the release at newsroom.bankofamerica.com under the Press Releases tab.) This survey assumes that these managers are representative of the average institutional investor, and have already positioned their portfolios to match their investors' views.

This survey is a good place to check one's own outlook against the institutional consensus. For instance, in August 2007 the U.S. and world markets were doing well. The Dow hit 14,000. At the time, the survey said that

- An increasing number of managers thought equities were undervalued.
- A net 41 percent of managers believed bonds were overvalued.
- Respondents saw wider credit spreads as a problem centering around the U.S. housing market, and saw emerging markets as relatively appealing. A net 29 percent (up sharply from 16 percent

the month before) said emerging markets offered the best corporate profit outlook.

- A net 29 percent were underweight on banks; a net 33 percent were overweight on technology.
- Asset allocators listed credit-default risk and counterparty risk as key potential risks.
- David Bowers, consultant to Merrill Lynch, commented that he continued to see market turmoil as "a credit and a financial event. Investors are not positioned for a spillover into the macro environment," he said.

This review gives real insight into what the professionals are thinking, recognizing that they can be just as wrong as anyone else. There are nuggets here, however—such as the point about counterparty risk—that may represent valid insight.

Yale Confidence Indexes

Well-known academic Robert Shiller has taught at Yale since 1982. He wrote the *New York Times* best seller *Irrational Exuberance* (Princeton University Press, 2000) and helped compile the popular Case-Shiller Home Price Indexes. In 1989, he began a semiannual (now monthly) survey that separately tracks individual and institutional investor opinions. The review, known on Yale's Web site as the Yale School of Management Stock Market Confidence Indexes, offers

- **One-Year Confidence Index**: Percent of respondents who think the market will rise in the upcoming twelve months.
- **Buy-on-Dips Confidence Index**: Percent who believe the market will rise the day after a hypothetical 3 percent drop in the Dow.
- **Crash Confidence Index**: Percent who believe there is a less than 10 percent chance that the market will avoid a crash during the next six months.
- **Valuation Confidence Index**: Percent of investors who believe the market is not too high (the percent answering "too low" or "about right" in relation to all votes).

Shiller's data shows a long-term shift in the number of investors ready to "buy the dip." During the 1991 recession, just 30 percent thought a 3 percent Dow drop was a buying opportunity. After years of

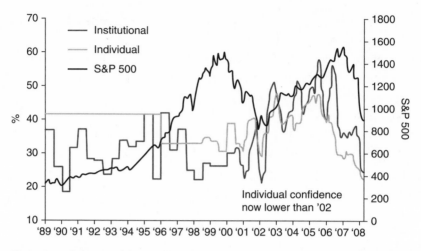

*Percentage of survey participants with confidence that there will be no stock market crash in the next 6 months.

Figure 7.4   Yale Crash Confidence Index, 1989–2008

Source: Bespoke Investment Group, Data from Robert Shiller

buy-the-dips success, the ratio stayed above 50 percent through the bear markets of 2001–2003 and 2008. Time will tell whether that trend reverses.

FIGURE 7.4 shows the Crash Confidence Index since the survey's 1989 inception. As the market hit highs in late 2007, investors became less confident in the market's ability to avoid a crash. Many investors, it seems, saw clouds on the horizon.

Also note the absolute low readings in 2002, which occurred *after* the market had already endured two years of declines. Investors recalled those repeated declines and likely projected that experience into the future. In retrospect, 2002 turned out to be a good time to *increase* stock market exposure.

Ned Davis Crowd Sentiment

Ned Davis Research, with more than one thousand—mostly institutional—clients is one of the most respected services examining historical market relationships. Its analysts attempt to put the current market into perspective and describe investment strategies that have done well in past, similar circumstances. Among other indicators, they track a proprietary combination of sentiment surveys (including those discussed in this chapter) and the options market signals discussed in Chapter 1. Charles Schwab customers have partial access to Ned Davis charts and research. Investors can also search the Internet for media references to Ned Davis, or see news reports at www.ndr.com.

University of Michigan Consumer Sentiment Index

Analysts use many economic indicators to predict the course of the economy, typically assuming that the market leads the economy by six to nine months. (The market might turn up half a year before current industrial output showed improvement, for instance.) In theory, good economic predictions should help traders improve portfolio performance.

Sadly, however, it's tough to make accurate, long-term economic readings and extrapolate them to market performance. The market is more volatile than the economy, an observation that led to the Wall Street old saw that "the stock market has predicted eight of the last five recessions."

Moreover, very few people are good at predicting either the economy or the market. A classic 1985 *Economist* magazine survey asked many different people to forecast various 1995 readings: the price of gold, interest rates, stock market performance, and so forth. Trash collectors and the chairmen of multinational corporations made the best guesses, outperforming former finance ministers and University of Oxford students.

The University of Michigan has been calling the same three hundred households each month since 1946 to ask for views on personal finances, business conditions, and purchasing power. Investors pay the most attention to this survey's index of consumer expectations. Consumers drive approximately 70 percent of economic activity, so traders expect that future buying patterns will be guided by consumer expectations.

FIGURE 7.5 shows the index of consumer expectations, which tends to mirror the stock market. Many traders look for divergences, zeroing in on times when consumer expectations improved but the market did not. When consumers feel better or worse than the market, they may know something that the market isn't factoring in.

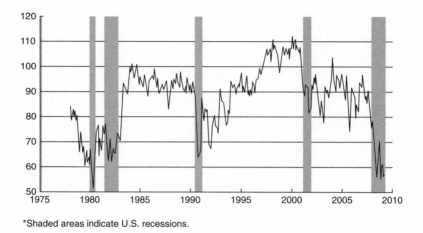

*Shaded areas indicate U.S. recessions.

Figure 7.5   University of Michigan sentiment survey

Source: Federal Reserve Bank of St. Louis

State Street Investor Confidence Index

State Street is a Boston financial services company that processes trades for a wide variety of global institutional investors. Their analysts see the daily trades that big investors make. In June 2000, State Street began aggregating movements in the $15 trillion in assets it holds as custodian for their institutional clients. State Street then determines if the asset shifts are largely defensive or offensive, making distinctions between U.S., European, and Asian markets. The result is a monthly reading, released the second-to-last Tuesday of each month, that summarizes institutional investor confidence.

FIGURE 7.6 shows the State Street Investor Confidence Index compared to the S&P 500, since its inception. Note that risk exposure was high throughout the 2000–2002 bear market, but dropped precipitously at the end of October 2008, a month when the market dropped 18 percent.

In August 2006, State Street started tracking confidence by region. The Asian and European levels did not fluctuate much, but the North American index moved substantially. The 2007 August top, for example, peaked at 116.5 (up from 95.8 for July 2007). There is not enough data to draw conclusions, but it is worth following. State Street posts the results at www.statestreet.com/ investor confidence index.

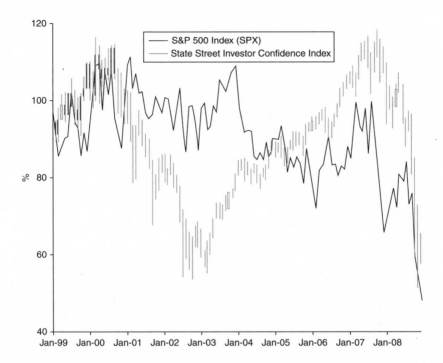

Figure 7.6 Monthly State Street Investor Confidence Index

Source: State Street via tradersnarrative.com

RESOURCES

Find current sentiment survey and asset allocation results for members of the American Association of Individual Investors (AAII) at http://www.aaii.com/research. Bloomberg and SentimenTrader also collect historical results for the survey.

Market Vane is a subscription service at www.marketvane.net.

Find the Yale School of Management Stock Market Confidence Indexes at http://icf.som.yale.edu/Confidence.Index or by googling "Yale market confidence."

Find the University of Michigan Consumer Sentiment Survey and other economic data, along with other economic studies, at the St. Louis Federal Reserve Web site at http://research.stlouisfed.org.

The State Street Investor Confidence Index is at www.statestreet.com. The monthly press release includes comments on trends and outlooks from State Street Associates.

The Trader's Narrative blog covers a wide variety of indicators, including a weekly summary of sentiment indicators, at www.tradersnarrative.com.

Chapter 8

Analyzing the Analysts

Analysts are supposed to be critics of corporations. They often end up being public relations spokesmen for them.

—RALPH WANGER, former chief investment officer
for the Columbia Acorn Fund

WALL STREET AS WE KNOW it may have disappeared in 2008. Bear Stearns, Lehman Brothers, and Merrill Lynch vaporized. The two remaining investment banks, Goldman Sachs and Morgan Stanley, turned themselves into chartered banks.

But though the Wall Street of years past is gone, Wall Street's function is very much a part of the present. For the most part, the titans of Wall Street still decide which firms have access to the public markets, controlling a large part of the capital that expanding companies need.

Those companies that reach the stock markets do so through an intersection of professionals and their firms. Bankers, consultants, and attorneys work on initial public offerings (IPOs). Analysts research stocks; portfolio managers buy what they like and sell or ignore what they don't. Collectively, the two create the consensual reality that is share value. Company management, for its part, works to build a successful company and generate profits. Each party in the process has its own set of incentives, motivations, and pressures.

This chapter will look at the interplay between investment bankers, analysts, portfolio managers, and company management to find signals that can help investors see around corners.

Investment bankers: call on private and public companies to suggest and then execute deals. In his play *Glengarry Glen Ross*, writer David Mamet coined the ABC rule, which stands for "always be closing." As a group, investment bankers follow this rule as they bring companies public, merge or sell firms, or raise debt financing. The more deals a banker closes, the better his pay and professional reputation.

Analysts: offer opinions about companies after an initial public offering. They help management make its best case to investors but must also guard their reputation for objectivity with portfolio managers. Analysts serve multiple masters: investment bankers, trading desks, portfolio managers, and company managements. Their role is inherently a conflicted one.

Management: tries to run a business efficiently, producing a profit that satisfies investors. In the past, a firm's owner was its management, and that's still the case in small companies. With the growth of private equity firms, even some larger companies are operated by their owners. For the most part, though, large companies trade publicly and employ professional managers to oversee and grow a business on behalf of its numerous owners, the stockholders.

Managers sell a product or service, and they also market the company's stock. Most provide a product or service, and let the stock price reflect their efforts. A few specifically promote themselves to potential investors.

Portfolio managers and stockholders: are a wide-ranging group, including mutual fund managers, pension fund managers, hedge fund managers, and retail investors. Despite their different profiles, all are under pressure to deliver investment results in an uncertain world. Each has specific benchmarks by which they gauge success or failure.

These participants make the markets run. Their particular motivations and constraints provide a range of market clues for the observant investor.

Smooth Performance in a Bumpy World— The Earnings Estimate

Portfolio managers put their careers in jeopardy if they hold a stock that crashes, or "blows up." They are paid to see these things coming, even in a naturally chaotic, volatile world. As a result, these managers pay premiums for companies with even earnings growth and no performance surprises.

To earn those premiums, management looking to curry favor with skittish portfolio managers may use the flexibility embedded in accounting standards. As much as they can, they "smooth" numbers from quarter to quarter, to emphasize the appearance of predictable stability. (A 2005 survey of four hundred executives done by University of Washington professor Shivaram Rajgopal found that 78 percent would sacrifice long-term investments for smoother earnings.)

Companies vary in their approach to publicly forecasting revenue and profits. Researchers at the University of Southern California suggest that firms that issue more predictions are more focused on meeting and exceeding investor expectations than are companies that give little or no guidance.

Firms that give less guidance, however, often spend more money on research and development than do their more talkative peers. Research and development costs are expensed in the quarter when they occur, so cutting a research budget is a quick way to meet an earnings estimate. Many savvy investors check to make sure that a company is spending enough money on research and development, rather than sacrifice this vital function.

Given these pressures, there are only two reasons for a company to fall short of a previously announced earnings estimate:

1. Management didn't make an accurate prediction. Normally, management makes conservative projections, with enough ongoing business to meet their publicly announced targets. Missed guidance means that things are worse than a conservative prediction suggests, or that they don't have operational control of the business.
2. Accounting flexibility is already overstretched, and there's nowhere to find another few pennies of quarterly earnings.

Neither possibility makes investors happy. The market can sharply punish a company for underperformance by as little as one penny. Similarly sized overperformance isn't typically met with the same degree of reward, however. A company must substantially outperform its earnings estimate to push stock values higher.

KB Home (KBH) is a good example of how the market issues rewards and punishments that are based on earnings. KB Home beat profit expectations for twenty-nine straight quarters from 1999 to 2007. The stock rose from $12 to $50 per share. Then the home-builder reported a loss of $1.93 on June 28, 2007. The stock price that day closed at $39.89. One year later, it stood at $17.72. It hit a low of $8 in late 2008, part of the brutal sell-off of homebuilder stocks as the housing crisis extended and deepened.

IT'S ALL ABOUT MARKETING

When a company doesn't issue earnings estimates, a stock analyst may do it instead, with or without company guidance. Analysts are charged with tracking management efforts and offering their opinions to investors.

A meeting with management is an analyst's first step in developing an earnings forecast. No one should know the industry and the company's outlook better than the people running it. This is especially true of the chief financial officer (CFO), the person in charge of the budgets, sales forecasts, and balance sheet management.

That doesn't mean, however, that managers always have a realistic vision of their company's future. **FIGURE 8.1** shows the results from the Duke University/CFO Magazine Business Outlook Survey. Every three months, Duke asks participants about their optimism for the economy (black line) and their own company (gray line) on a 1 to 100 scale. Generally, CFOs are more—sometimes much more—optimistic about the prospects for their own firms than for the economy at large.

The survey measures whether CFOs are more or less optimistic than during the previous quarter. Coming out of the 2001–2002 downturn, survey results improved along with business conditions. Starting in 2004, the pace of increasing optimism reached a climax. Over time, those good feelings began to wane. Business got gradually tougher, and by late 2005 an even number of CFOs were either more or less optimistic than they had been during the previous

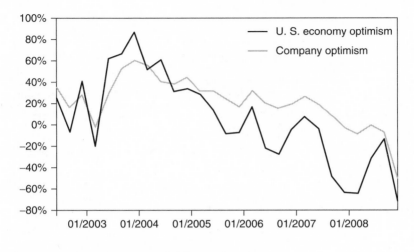

Figure 8.1   Duke University CFO survey

Source: Duke University/*CFO* Magazine Global Business Outlook Survey

quarter. By the beginning of 2008, the CFO survey reflected an increasingly difficult operating environment. Analysts, of course, must choose what they will believe.

Investment bankers employ analysts, but institutional investors ultimately pay for the analyst's work. If they feel the analyst's efforts and insights are helpful, they direct more of their trading to the brokerage firm that employs the analyst. *Institutional Investor (II)* magazine polls portfolio managers every year, asking which analyst was best in each market sector. Being named best in class is a big deal. The honor gives an analyst better access to those who manage the companies they analyze, and typically boosts compensation and professional reputation as well.

Analysts increase the possibility that they'll be named best in their sector by being available to their largest customers to discuss industry developments, and by providing specific information about a company that may not appear in its public report. For instance, an analyst might call a key client and say, "I hear XYZ's supplier is having trouble with a key module of the new product set to launch next month. I have my doubts about them hitting their release date." They also curry favor with their best clients by getting them one-on-one time with management, to ask their own questions and gauge the answers without other investors around. At the end of the day, portfolio managers care less about analyst's target price and earnings estimate than about access to in-depth sector knowledge and management.

When an analyst issues a negative opinion, he or she puts that access at risk, and may encounter a significant set of headaches. Clients with big positions will likely be upset. Company managers won't be happy, either. They've spent valuable time discussing the firm's bright future with someone who didn't agree. They'll be less likely to offer that time in the future, to either the analyst or the analyst's clients. In most cases, it's easier for an analyst to stick with consensus numbers, which are typically equal or close to those that a company's management provides.

When a respected analyst faces this prospect and submits a downgrade anyway, the market notices. Participants know that the analyst needs an airtight case for making a negative call. By the same token, it's not easy for an analyst to buck group opinion and find value in a particularly downtrodden equity. In either case, one analyst can have a huge effect on stock price.

ONE WAY OR THE OTHER

Good analysts are extremely knowledgeable, spending long hours doing channel checks, reviewing product launches, and crunching reams of numbers. Some make their names through management access; others build a reputation for extraordinary follow-through with clients.

A third group looks for an unfilled niche, often taking a position as the contrary analyst who points out potential problems. They're usually the first to ask pointed questions on the quarterly earnings conference call. But they do offer a great deal of value to portfolio managers, by providing a necessary counterweight to management's natural bullishness.

Meredith Whitney, a former banking analyst at Oppenheimer who has started her own firm, is well known for her willingness to point out problems. In October 2007, she forcefully announced that Citigroup had balance sheet issues and predicted that it would need to raise capital and cut or even eliminate its dividend. Management protested but, sure enough, three months later Citigroup was forced to cut its dividend.

HIDING THEIR TRUE FEELINGS

If an analyst does harbor serious doubts, the fate of analyst Henry Blodget offers a reason to publicly speak up.

Investors remember Blodget for being bullish in public while expressing doubts to colleagues and major clients. Blodget burst on the scene with his October 1998 call on Amazon.com (AMZN), predicting it would go from $175 to $400 per share. It did. In three weeks it blew through the $400 target and continued to rocket, approaching $1,000 in January 1999 (split-adjusted). The call propelled Blodget into the big leagues. Merrill Lynch hired him away from Oppenheimer, where he had become a favored analyst for the investment banking group.

Despite publicly warning that there would only be a few long-term survivors in the gold rush era of Internet stocks, Blodget bowed to pressure and issued bullish forecasts and "buy" recommendations for many of those companies. In private e-mails to colleagues, he characterized firms 24/7 Media, Excite@Home, and InfoSpace as "shit," "crap," and "junk." When then New York Attorney General Eliot Spitzer found the e-mails, Blodget became the poster boy for all that was wrong with Wall Street's marketing machine.

In the fallout, Wall Street collectively paid a $1.4 billion fine and promised to strengthen the physical and intellectual separation between research and investment banking. Company management was also held to tougher standards. Under Regulation Fair Disclosure, or Reg FD, management is now required to make any meaningful news available first to the full public, without first leaking juicy tidbits to favored analysts. (Interestingly, Reg FD pushed many executives toward revealing information only in quarterly earnings announcements that are vetted by staff lawyers. Rather than open the flow of information, it closed it down.)

Blodget went on to reinvent himself as a highly regarded blogger. In a December 2008 interview with *Wired* magazine, Blodget commented on his new freedom to speak his mind. "On Wall Street, I'd consistently submit a report that would say, 'This is going to be roadkill,' and it would come back rewritten as 'We see some weakness,'" Blodget says. "Now I can say, 'It's going to be roadkill.' That's very satisfying."

REVISING ESTIMATES

Wall Street follows earnings estimates, but investors are even more interested in the direction of estimate revisions, carefully following whether analysts and management are raising or lowering projections. Management is motivated to produce a smooth earnings stream—and analysts earn penalties if their projections are wrong and far from the consensus—but the business world naturally produces both fat and lean periods. The dual pressures can lead to a pattern that usually goes like this:

1. Company enters a good stretch with new product introduction, or general industry prospects improve.
2. Company beats estimates and says on the earnings conference call that the future looks pretty good. The analysts keep their forecasts unchanged or bump them up modestly as they await confirmation of business momentum in future quarters.
3. Company continues to do well. It reports strong numbers and positive firm prospects. Analysts raise their forecasts. At this point, their target price may be lagging the actual stock price.
4. Company rides the growth wave and profits handsomely. Analysts aggressively raise earnings targets. They've looked too timid for a while now, so they set target prices far in front of the current stock price.
5. Company's growth starts to slow. They're still beating estimates, but perhaps inventory is starting to build. Analysts see it as a bump in the road but the stock price takes a hit. Growth stock investors suspect the firm's growth phase is coming to an end and sell. Analysts maintain earnings estimates.
6. Company proves the glitch was a temporary hiccup and is back on the desired growth trajectory, which is getting steeper in order to maintain investor enthusiasm.
7. Or the company misses its forecast. Perhaps it withdraws financial projections or says that "visibility" is poor. Stock values drop sharply. Analysts cut their estimates slightly, but publicly defend the stock price reaction as overdone. They portray the sell-off as a buying opportunity for the patient, long-term investor.
8. The company's heady growth, and likely the industry's, has come to an end for the cycle. Analyst estimates continue to be missed and are cut. The stock continues to drift lower in fits and starts.

Analysts, having been burned for a few quarters now, drastically reduce their expectations and cut their public recommendation to a hold, which is shorthand for "sell," or even to a sell, which is shorthand for "short" if you're a hedge fund client.

9. At some point, the company misses even these reduced analyst estimates, and the stock goes up. All the bad news is priced into the stock. Or the company beats expectations and revives market interest. This classic growth cycle normally happens just once for a company; it's unusual to have a firm reinvent itself and repeat a cycle of rapid and sustained growth.

Buy Side versus Sell Side

Every street has two sides, and Wall Street is no different. Large investing institutions, including hedge funds, mutual funds, pension funds, and insurance firms are commonly called the buy side. Firms such as investment banks, brokerages, and boutique research companies comprise the sell side. These firms provide stock recommendations (buy, sell, or hold) and usually have other deal-oriented functions, such as underwriting securities or executing trades.

Investment banks employ analysts and make their opinions public, so reported commentary mostly comes from the sell side. Buy-side firms consider the views of sell-side analysts, but they also employ their own analysts to develop an internal view and opinion. If a buy-side analyst comes across key information, he discusses it only within the firm.

Buy-side analysts are out of the public eye and do not work under the pressures facing sell-side analysts, so their opinions are often more highly regarded by their employers. A portfolio manager is more likely to listen to his internal analyst than to act on a sell-side report that's sitting on his desk.

In that tendency, however, he may be wrong. Boris Groysberg, Paul Healy, and Craig Chapman, all of Harvard Business School, challenged that assumption in their paper "Buy-Side vs. Sell-Side Analysts' Earnings Forecasts," published in the July–August 2008 issue of the *Financial Analysts Journal*. They found the buy-side earnings forecasts were an average 8 to16 percent *higher* than those on the sell-side, and the forecast errors were 11 to 15 percent *greater*. The difference, they concluded, was because sell-side companies often have better analysts than do their buy-side colleagues, and because sell-side analysts are in constant competition with one another.

It's not easy to know who to believe. As Blodget found, analysts serve multiple masters. The best way to benefit from their hard work is to pay attention to their industry overview and specific company information. Tap into their expertise, but don't rely on their earnings estimates or price targets. When possible, read the entire report and look between the lines to imagine how the analyst may be pulling punches. What would the analyst say over a couple of beers, rather than in a report that's carefully vetted by lawyers?

Consider, too, how accurate an analyst has been in the past. StarMine is a research subsidiary of Thomson Reuters that tracks analyst accuracy. To warn of vulnerable high-flying stocks, StarMine flags situations in which a highly rated analyst projects earnings below the market consensus. They may be too early, or even wrong, but it's wise to consider the opinion of a recognized expert who strays from the consensus view.

TRACKING REVISIONS

Zacks Investment Research collects and analyzes company guidance and analyst estimates. It places a premium on highlighting instances in which companies greatly exceed or miss estimates, as such trends are usually underappreciated and last longer than many expect.

Zacks also calculates a total revisions ratio for the overall market and individual sectors. A reading below 0.8 is bearish (more than five negative revisions for every four positive); a reading above 1.25 is bullish. Find an ongoing commentary on earnings revisions at www.zacks.com.

TABLE 8.1 shows the revision ratios by sector as of January 15, 2009. It suggested that the market would have a difficult time advancing as analysts continued to lower their forecasts. Investors using this approach want to be in the market (and especially in the sectors) when data suggests that analysts are behind, changing estimates to keep pace with actual company performance.

Aggregated analyst projections can show the overall revision trend. **FIGURE 8.2** shows the actual earnings change for the S&P 500 and the trend of analyst forecasts. The analysts tended to be

Table 8.1   Zacks report of earnings for the week of January 15, 2009

	Average 4-wk EPS Change (FY09)	Revisions Ratio	Firms with FY09 EPS Increase	Firms with FY09 EPS Decrease
Consumer Staple	−1.27%	0.33	8	25
Consumer Discretionary	−3.20%	0.25	16	60
Utilities	−1.39%	0.25	4	27
Energy	−7.68%	0.21	3	36
Health Care	−1.18%	0.17	11	39
Materials	−12.03%	0.14	2	26
Technology	−6.91%	0.11	8	57
Financial Services	−8.78%	0.10	6	72
Telecom	−4.42%	0.10	1	8
Industrials	−5.18%	0.06	4	50
S&P 500	−5.24%	0.16	63	400

Source: Zacks.com

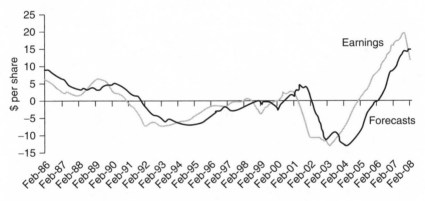

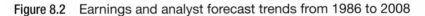

Figure 8.2   Earnings and analyst forecast trends from 1986 to 2008

Source: James Montier 'Mind Matters' April 2008 strategy essay

consistently behind the trend and were slow to recognize the change in actual earnings (on the way up in 2003 and on the way down in late 2007). In broad terms, it's best to bet more aggressively on the market when actual earnings are accelerating, and especially when analyst forecasts lag reality (or vice versa).

MARKET STRATEGISTS

The Zacks analysis aggregates all the analysts' reporting on individual companies. This is known as bottom-up analysis.

Another approach involves looking at the big factors affecting business: inflation, interest rates, and demographic trends, among others. This is a top-down approach for market forecasting. Most brokerage firms have investment strategists who are well versed in these macroeconomic factors. They consider historical trends and look for pieces of data that suggest economic strength or weakness, often before many businesses themselves are aware of it.

For instance, former Fed chairman Alan Greenspan started his career as an economic analyst at The Conference Board, a New York City think tank. One of his favorite statistics was the number of corrugated boxes being ordered and produced. Firms ordering boxes were receiving orders, he reasoned. As went the boxes, so went the economy.

Strategists use these macroeconomic inputs to forecast earnings for the market as a whole. They produce statements that might say, "We forecast next year's S&P 500 earnings at $70 per share. We expect inflation to be in check and the ten-year Treasury to yield 4 percent. Accordingly, we are estimating a market multiple of 15 and fair value for the S&P of 1050." Like an analyst's price target, these targets are less useful than the report itself, which may reveal insightful trends or warnings.

Strategists also suggest sector weightings. Many investors review the high-level arguments for and against various sectors, looking for well-rounded opinions that stray from the consensus.

S&P Analysts versus Wall Street Strategists

The turn of the year is a natural time to review the past year and look to the upcoming twelve months, attempting to forecast the market's likely direction. Bloomberg collects year-end estimates from strategists. The group is usually collectively bullish. They are employed by investment banks, which have a vested business interest in seeing their clients involved in the stock market. Consciously or not, they pressure strategists to make the best case for a healthy market. **TABLE 8.2** shows the collective forecast (as of December 31, 2008) for where the S&P 500 would end 2009.

Standard & Poor's analysts are under less business pressure to paint a sunny picture. Their sector analysts try to accurately forecast

Table 8.2   Wall Street strategists' S&P 500 2009 forecasts

Firm	Strategist	2009 Price Target	Expected 2009 % change
UBS	David Bianco	1,300	43.9
Deutsche Bank	Binky Chadha	1,140	26.2
Goldman Sachs	David Kostin	1,100	21.8
Strategas	Jason Trennert	1,100	21.8
JPMorgan Chase	Thomas Lee	1,100	21.8
Credit Suisse	Andrew Garthwaite	1,050	16.2
Citigroup	Tobias Levkovich	1,000	10.7
HSBC	Kevin Gardiner	1,000	10.7
JPMorgan Chase	Abhijit Chakrabortti	975	7.9
Merrill Lynch	Richard Bernstein	975	7.9
Barclays	Barry Knapp	874	-3.2
	Average	1,056	16.9

Source: Bespoke Investment Group Via Bloomberg

Table 8.3   S&P analyst forecast for 2009 of aggregate S&P 500 earnings

March 20, 2008	$81.52
April 9, 2008	$72.60
June 25, 2008	$70.13
August 29, 2008	$64.66
September 10, 2008	$58.87
October 14, 2008	$48.52
January 2, 2009	$42.26!

Source: frontlinethoughts.com

S&P 500 *earnings* for the upcoming year. (They don't forecast an actual S&P 500 trading level.) **TABLE 8.3** shows S&P's collective 2009 earnings forecast through the course of 2008; it's hard to miss the constant, pervasive, and dramatic revisions they made as 2008 progressed. Without making broad market predictions, the earnings forecast downgrades shouted that business was deteriorating. It was up to investors to decide if these estimates were realistic and, if so, whether the market was correctly pricing these estimates.

Consider one simple exercise to see how an investor might have used available information to create a course of action. Take the S&P 500 earnings estimate, which has a history of being the more accurate, and assume that it is accurate. Next, decide what market multiple to assign to the $42.62 expected earnings, perhaps by looking to history for an answer. Ned Davis, owner of Ned Davis Research and a prominent interpreter of historical patterns and data, has found that the historical market multiple of *trough* earnings is 18.8.

Applying an 18.8 multiple to these trough estimates produces an estimate of 801 (18.8 × $42.62) for the S&P 500's level at the end of 2009. The S&P touched 750 in early November 2008, so one could argue the market had reached a low and was appropriately looking forward. The S&P 500 ended 2008 at 903. A less optimistic forecast for earnings recovery might conclude that the market would not easily move forward from 900, and could slip back to between 750 and 800 as that reality set in among investors. In March 2009, the S&P 500 did decline to under 700 before rebounding.

None of this is gospel, but it's better to be approximately right than exactly wrong. In this case, looking at the S&P earnings forecast and giving them the benefit of the doubt over the investment bank strategists would lead to a more nuanced outlook.

RESOURCES

StarMine is an institutional research product but has a variety of free newsletters available on its Web site www.starmine.com.

Zacks has a variety of freely available and subscription tools on its Web site www.zacks.com. Zacks' revision ratio is profiled in a weekly "Earnings Trends" column.

The historical and estimated S&P 500 earnings data can be found at http://www2.standardandpoors.com/spf/xls/index/SP500EPSEST.XLS. Howard Silverblatt, senior index analyst for S&P, compiles this data and often offers his interpretation of the data to varying media outlets, which can be captured by setting a Google Alert for "Howard Silverblatt."

John Mauldin writes a weekly market commentary titled "Thoughts from the Frontline," freely available at www.frontlinethoughts.com.

Many good books discuss the role of analysts on Wall Street; of particular interest are Andy Kessler's *Wall Street Meat* and Stephen McClellan's *Full of Bull*. Both outline their experiences as well-regarded sell-side analysts.

Reporting the Financial News, Gauging the Investor's Psyche

The man who reads nothing at all is better educated than the man who reads nothing but newspapers.

—THOMAS JEFFERSON

Charlie and I love newspapers—we each read five a day—and believe that a free and energetic press is a key ingredient for maintaining a great democracy.

—WARREN BUFFETT, in his 2006 annual letter to shareholders

BACK TO THE TIME of smoke signals, people have wanted to hear the news. There's a sense of community in knowing who is doing what and where one stands among the crowd. Thomas Jefferson hated the media for the lies—and occasional inconvenient truth—it spread in his day. Modern-day investors consume hours of media every day in attempts to track the progress of an increasingly complex and interconnected world. Between television, radio, and print, media outlets offer an astonishing amount of financial and market information.

Some of that information is vital, reporting key company news and industry developments. The best journalists also report on developing trends, which tend to evolve over months or years.

The daily buzz of financial reports also contains a fair amount of "noise": information that's not especially important, or has taken on exaggerated significance.

In his book *The User Illusion* (Penguin, 1999), Danish scientist Tor Nørretranders notes that the human mind consciously processes just sixteen of the eleven million bits of information our senses collect every second. The brain naturally filters out what it deems unimportant. The world economy and stock market also bombard the senses with an overwhelming amount of data, information it's impossible to fully intellectually consume.

Like diners following conversations in a crowded restaurant, investors need reliable ways to determine which market moves are unimportant noise, which are significant signals, and whether other market participants have interpreted that information in similar ways. By doing their own homework and independently filtering the market, investors can find instances where the market diverges from the prevailing outlook, which may lead to superior investing opportunities.

Magazine Covers

Television stations, newspapers, and magazines cannot stay in business without selling advertising space; many of them also need subscription income. (Even magazines that offer free subscriptions track their readership, because they can charge higher advertising rates when more people read them.) They lure subscribers and advertisers by offering the journalism they believe will be of most interest to their target audiences. Sometimes that means being first with a story, though it can also mean offering the most complete or most insightful take on an event. Television, newspaper, and magazine journalists work with editors and fact-checkers, as well as under a professional code of ethics, with a goal of producing stories that are both accurate and fair.

Headlines, including magazine covers, help attract readers' attention. Headlines can also help sell magazines, particularly when they seem to confirm a popularly held view. But by the time a magazine puts a widely held viewpoint on the cover, the market has probably already figured out that particular wrinkle—and priced it in.

Researchers Tom Arnold, John Earl, and David North of the University of Richmond confirmed that idea in an article titled "Are Cover Stories Effective Contrarian Indicators?" in the

March–April 2007 issue of the *Financial Analysts Journal*. The trio collected twenty years of cover headlines from *BusinessWeek*, *Fortune*, and *Forbes* and classified them as positive, negative, or neutral. They found that positive covers tend to signal the end of superior performance and negative ones the end of poor performance. If the news is clear enough to make the cover, it is likely already priced by the market; and the underlying trend, good or bad, has a good chance of reversing.

It's easy to get caught up in the headline of the moment. Fidelity Investments has a chart room with a wall devoted to magazine covers. It serves as a reminder that the current consensus opinion is often wrong, and that the future often confounds the projections.

The Big Weeklies

Weekly publications that cover ideas and trends around the nation and world are arguably the magazines with the broadest reach. They cover a wide variety of topics, from health to politics to motion pictures, typically devoting a page or two to business news. Unlike the readers of *Forbes* or the *Economist*, *Time* and *Newsweek* readers don't look to these publications for in-depth, extensive market or business coverage.

A prominent broadleaf magazine's cover story on a specific company or sector serves notice that a trend has moved from the business world and onto the larger society's radar screen. These pieces often herald the end of whatever phenomenon they describe. *Time's* June 13, 2005 cover titled "Home $weet Home," featured a story about the wide-spread popularity for real estate. A housing downturn began within weeks of the story.

Time's 1999 Person of the Year was Amazon.com founder Jeff Bezos. Amazon's stock had rocketed by more than 5,000 percent in the previous three years, and the original online bookseller was moving into housewares and power tools. By the time the magazine acknowledged Bezos's brilliance with the headline "E-Commerce is Changing the Way the World Shops," the stock had found its peak, falling by 85 percent over the next two years.

Reading the Paper

The newspaper equivalent of a magazine cover is known as "above the fold": the top half of the front page that's seen through newsstand boxes. It typically offers the stories editors feel are most important and will best capture reader attention.

The *New York Times* is the newspaper equivalent of *Time* magazine; the motto printed at the top of every day's paper says "All the news that's fit to print." Headlines above the fold are typically about politics or world events, though business events do sometimes appear here. Stories about the market itself are relatively rare, and are often left to the *Wall Street Journal*. When the *New York Times* runs a big story about the stock market, you can be sure that most market participants have already noticed the event or trend that the story reports, and have adjusted their trades accordingly.

Across town at the *Wall Street Journal*, writers and editors primarily focus on business and the markets. Front-page stories normally report the news, quoting a few experts on the matter at hand. Every once in a while, though, an underlying market opinion seeps onto the front page. This signal isn't as obvious as a *New York Times* headline, but the story leaves the reader wondering "how do they *know?*" and "why is *this* on the front page?" The *Wall Street Journal*'s headlines can also signal that a trend is at or near its peak.

Barry Ritholtz noticed this in his Big Picture blog on May 23, 2007, when he commented on a *Wall Street Journal* page-one story headlined "Why Market Optimists Say this Bull Has Legs." He wrote, "Today's *Wall Street Journal* has a very bullish, front-page article on the current bull market lasting another decade or so. In the past, that has operated as a bit of a warning sign that an intermediate top was nearing." The market continued its uneven climb, but eighteen months later the S&P 500 was down 44 percent.

It can be dangerous to look for a "sign" in every story, but it is helpful to think about why a story is on the front page or cover. Its prominence may mean that the outlook is widely held, and therefore already priced into the market.

RULE OF PAGE SIXTEEN

Donald Coxe, a former global strategist for BMO Financial Group, uses the newspaper to gauge how media professionals are noticing important trends. He advises to invest, not based on what's on page one, but based on important stories buried deep inside the paper.

In August 2007, food prices were rising substantially and Coxe's analysis showed there were serious, long-lasting supply/demand imbalances. The story was buried on the inner pages of the paper. Coxe told traders that investments in fertilizer, seed, and farm equipment companies were underappreciated and would do well. In the months to follow, food prices continued to rise and there were serious worldwide shortages. In May 2008, countries responded by rationing such basic staples as rice. Even without problems in the United States, some Costco stores were forced to ration their rice supplies. People feared the worst.

Food prices surged, shortages made the front page, and Don Coxe continued to make the case for a long-term bull market in agriculture. High investor interest spurred the opening of the Coxe Commodity Strategy Fund, which raised $300 million.

Eventually, however, traders priced the shortages into the market. In the next six months, crop yields were higher than expected, and a global slowdown crimped both credit and demand. Fertilizer firm Mosaic (MOS), which advanced 300 percent from August 2007 to May 2008, fell by 75 percent, to below its August 2007 level.

The Funny Pages

Comic artists don't typically draw material from SEC findings or company conference calls. They look at the world around them in search of absurdity and humor. When comic artists do find good material in the business world, it's another sign that an established trend may be peaking.

For a case in point, consider oil, which saw unprecedented price increases during the summer of 2008. A few months earlier, it had broken $100 per barrel. Some were calling for $200 a barrel by the end of the year, and perhaps $500 a barrel by the end of the decade. Sports utility vehicle owners unsuccessfully tried to trade their gas-guzzlers for smaller economy cars; Congress held hearings on whether the oil market was being manipulated by unscrupulous speculators. On July 22, 2008, with oil at $128 a barrel, a comic strip called *Wizard of Id* used oil as its punch line, suggesting that the commodity was too expensive to heat and pour on castle invaders.

In hindsight, oil had peaked the prior week at $145. Six months later, with recession sapping demand and speculators unwinding their bullish bets, oil was at $50 and heading lower. The market had reversed another long, sustained trend.

Late Night Talk Shows

Watch monologues offered by Conan O'Brien on the *Tonight Show* or Jon Stewart on the *Daily Show*. If they take pokes at the financial markets, you'll know that a trend may be hitting its peak. In the midst of the October 2008 market crash, for instance, Stewart mocked CNBC's decision to put ten (!) market pundits on the air at the same time, all commenting on why stocks were getting hammered. Stewart felt that hysteria had reached a fevered—and funny—pitch. When comics ask, "Have we lost our minds?" it can be good to step back and see if they may be right.

CNBC Highlight

If an item has its own CNBC box, it's at the forefront of many investors' minds. When gold rocketed toward $1,000 per ounce in spring 2007, the network's box detailed every penny price change. When oil moved towards $100 per barrel in summer 2008, CNBC highlighted every blip.

Jim Rogers, a well-known portfolio manager and long-time commodity bull, has commented that he'll know it's time to sell his commodity positions when CNBC stops reporting from the floor of the New York Stock Exchange in favor of the NYMEX (New York Mercantile Exchange).

That said, CNBC does find topic experts and conducts some terrifically insightful interviews. But the power of the Internet allows one to watch those clips in isolation, gleaning the most useful information in perhaps ten minutes a day. Bloomberg Television also brings very knowledgeable professionals on the air and is generally known for having a more staid, nonpromotional approach. They also keep a video archive worth reviewing on a regular basis. Find interview links on Bloomberg.com and CNBC.com, or look for the interviews blog authors found most interesting.

The Internet—Real Time Tracking

No need to wait for the morning paper or the weekly magazine when everyone is discussing a topic on the Internet. The Web's democratic style lets anyone broadcast opinions via a Web log, usually known as a blog.

Matt Drudge, keeper of the Drudge Report (drudgereport.com), was one of the earliest bloggers. He scans newspapers from around the world and posts links to stories he feels are important, bizarre, or merely entertaining. Sometimes he breaks stories, typically discussing a rumor or leak that can't be confirmed to a newspaper editor's satisfaction.

When a market event dominates the Drudge Report headlines, it's another signal that a well-established trend may be reaching a climax. One example involves the morning of January 22, 2008, when the Dow had fallen on previous days on continued concern about the credit markets. Even before the open, the Drudge's headline was "The Panic of 2008 . . . Dow Set to Drop 500." It turned out to be the culmination of a tough intermediate stretch for the markets, as the market dropped hundreds of points on the open, but then regained most of its early losses.

Tracking What People Are Searching

LexisNexis is a subscription-based service best known for its database of legal opinions, which lawyers use to research cases and arguments. (Full disclosure: the author interned there in the late 1980s). The database also electronically stores hundreds of newspapers and other print media, and makes articles available for search and retrieval.

The news-retrieval arm, known as Nexis, has a feature that lets customers see what topics are most searched and/or written about. Nexis can help investors understand what topics have recently captured editors' attention, and point toward trends that are nearing their peak.

Google Trends

Google Trends (google.com/trends) takes advantage of Google's database record of every user search. Investors can use this free data to see how popular a particular search term has been. Like Nexis, Google also charts the frequency with which a word or phrase has appeared in news stories collected by the Google news feature. Again, frequency can point to a trend that is reaching its sell-by date.

FIGURE 9.1 shows the 2007 Google Trend U.S. user volume results for the keywords "stock market." Note the two spikes. The most prominent (A) occurred on February 28, as oil rose to $100 per barrel and government reports signaled a slowing economy. The market had dropped 3.5 percent the prior day; the search surge likely

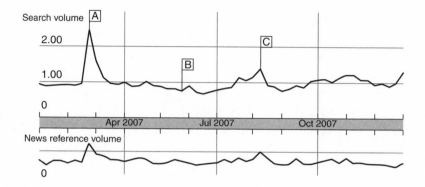

Figure 9.1   Google Trend results for stock market, 2007

Source: Google Trends

represents individuals looking for logic behind the dip. The market took a few bumpy weeks to digest the large decline, but within a few months had rebounded 10 percent from the February 27 close.

Traders can also use Google Trends to determine whether a fad is maintaining momentum or losing steam. Heely's (HLYS) introduced kids' shoes with wheels in their soles. For a while these were very popular, and the company came public in November 2007 to great acclaim. The IPO was priced at $21 per share but immediately ran up to nearly $35 as investors were excited about the terrific sales growth. Once the novelty wore off, Heely's failed to find an equally successful replacement product. Its stock suffered and traded down to $6 just one year after its IPO. Google Trends, inventory and pricing levels at online shoe retailer Zappos.com, and asking kids about the shoes' popularity could help spot the point at which the footwear lost its allure.

Twitter

Twitter is a Web-based instant messaging application allowing users to send a short message (under one hundred and forty characters) to everyone signed up to "follow" that user. President Obama used Twitter to reach more than fifty thousand people while on the campaign trail. Twitter also has a search feature (search.twitter.com) that lets users search for the most-used words or terms. The success of social network sites such as Facebook, LinkedIn, and Twitter, among others, increasingly allows investors to share and debate their best ideas.

RESOURCES

Barry Ritholtz is a widely read blogger who also posts many guests views he finds interesting at www.ritholtz.com.

Jeff Matthews wrote of the irony of the *Wizard of Id* commenting on the high price of oil in a July 23, 2008, post titled "How We Know Oil is Going Down." His blog is at http://jeffmatthewsisnotmakingthisup.blogspot.com.

Search for volume results for given terms at www.google.com/trends. An ongoing top listing of current search terms is provided at http://www.google.com/trends/hottrends. A similar function for Twitter is available at http://search.twitter.com.

Chapter 10

Sitting and Watching

You only find out who is swimming naked when the tide goes out.
—WARREN BUFFETT, in his 2001 annual letter to shareholders

We look for certain behavior patterns in management that are consistent with an efficient and prudent guardianship of our assets. If we visit a fan manufacturer in Texas and the CEO meets us at the airport in his Lexus, spends five hours with us, and then takes us out to an expensive restaurant and buys $300 bottles of wine, that is suggestive of somebody who isn't as prudent as we would like.
—J. CARLO CANNELL, portfolio manager, 2006 interview in
Value Investor Insight

THE HEART OF CAPITALISM lies in finding an unmet need, providing a solution, and then keeping ahead of competitive offerings that may be cheaper, better, or faster. Staying on top requires constant vigilance and continued good judgment.

From the outside, it can be difficult to tell whether management is making good choices. Decisions made today affect the profits of tomorrow. Should this research project be funded to completion or killed? Should we introduce this new product? A few big decisions and a thousand small ones determine a company's future.

Investors may not be able to vet every management choice, but they can watch for clues to how a company's management makes decisions and treats shareholder capital. If the visible decisions appear to be wise, the logic goes, it's likely that other, less visible decisions are also carefully considered.

An example lies in the famous $800 toilet seats purchased by the Pentagon during the 1980s. The price was a sign of endemic waste—and managerial incompetence—throughout the system. In this chapter, we'll discuss ways that investors can search for overpriced toilet seats, and their more recent equivalents, as they research potential trades.

Gone Fishing

Michelle Leder is an award-winning financial journalist who scans company SEC findings for tidbits, buried deep in the text, that reveal what management is doing with the shareholders' money. Most of the time, she finds information about executive compensation, options grants, and perks such as company cars or country club memberships.

Sometimes her search reveals more bizarre items. A November 25, 2008 post starts with this excerpt from a proxy filing for A. Schulman (SHLM).

> During fiscal 2008, the Compensation Committee determined that maintaining a lease on a private airplane was no longer a cost-effective method for providing business-related transportation to our Named Executive Officers and Directors. The airplane was used only for business-related travel, and personal use was not permitted. With the termination of the lease on the airplane, it also became increasingly difficult and cost prohibitive to access our Canadian fish camp. Consequently, the fish camp, which was only used for business entertainment purposes, was offered for sale during 2008. The only offer to purchase the fish camp came from Terry L. Haines, our former Chief Executive Officer and President. Ultimately, we negotiated with Mr. Haines to sell the fish camp for a purchase price of $55,000 and the transaction closed during fiscal 2009.

And Leder's reaction:

> There's so much to poke at here I almost don't know where to begin: The leased airplane for business purposes only? The fishing camp in Canada? The fact that the airplane was no longer necessary because the fish camp was sold? The sale of the fishing camp to the former CEO? The bargain basement price? Clearly, this is in the running for footnote of the year.

Leder's post also noted that two activist investor groups had positions in the firm and were pushing for significant change. If a good business is being grossly mismanaged, new management can lead to great returns on equity.

Other investors can also use Leder's technique, taking a close look at company filings and noticing whether the firm's management shows good judgment.

Consider, too, the timing and content of press releases and SEC reports. Former longtime financial journalist Herb Greenberg notes that some firms report bad news on Friday nights, hoping that no one will notice. Greenberg, who is now a principal at the stock research firm Greenberg Merit Research & Analytics, has also compared company press releases with conference call statements, which are part of SEC filings. Management has less latitude in what and how it discloses information to the SEC. Take notice if something important is in a filing, which few investors carefully read, not in the widely read press release.

Noted short seller Jim Chanos found references to company transactions with "related parties" buried deeply in Enron's 1999 10-K filing. Companies should not conduct official business within their own management teams; the temptation to line pockets at shareholder expense is just too great. The "related party" references cited an off-balance sheet liability, hiding operations that then-CFO Andrew Fastow was operating at great personal profit. The *Fortune* 500 list ranked Enron as the eighth-largest company in America; the following year, Enron entered bankruptcy, largely as a result of those hidden liabilities. The filing offered early signals that the outwardly strong company was rotting from the inside.

Executive Departures

Executives come, executives go—and the savvy investor can gather clues from those arrivals and departures. Jeff Skilling was a smart, hard-charging executive at consultant McKinsey & Company before he joined Enron in 1990. He helped transform Enron from a solid but unspectacular pipeline business into a freewheeling energy trader and developer. As the company grew, Ken Lay "promoted" himself from CEO to chairman and handed Skilling the reins. Skilling was forty-seven years old.

It was a shock when, six months later, Skilling announced that he was retiring. He denied rumored health problems. Ken Lay stepped back into the CEO's position. The outside world saw an odd but relatively harmless executive shuffle.

Behind the scenes, however, many of the deals that Skilling had pushed in pursuit of lofty quarterly earnings were beginning to fall apart. Largely unaware of the details, Lay didn't seem motivated to investigate. Enron descended into chaos and filed bankruptcy on December 2, 2001, four months after Skilling's surprise resignation.

Well-run companies have a good bench of executives running important divisions and working toward the CEO's office. Transitions tend to be gradual, with handoffs communicated to traders in advance. Alarm bells should ring in an investor's mind when a CEO or CFO suddenly departs. The alarm should get louder if that person is in the prime of his or her career, and shriller still if the departure is quietly noted in an SEC filing, but not announced by press release.

It takes a great deal of talent, hard work, and motivation to reach the executive suite, and those who arrive don't normally make sudden decisions to spend more time with their families or work on their golf games. It's much more likely that they've been pushed out for poor performance, are leaving on their own because they don't like what is going on, or are departing because they don't want to be around when a ticking time bomb detonates.

The Celebrity CEO's Exit

Watch out when a celebrity CEO steps down, riding off into the sunset in a blaze of glory. Celebrated CEOs, loved by Wall Street and mainstream media alike, typically leave after a long, sustained string of powerful business results.

But at its core, business is chaotic, unruly, and unpredictable, with inevitable bumps in the road. The departing CEO may have used legitimate accounting adjustments to pave over those potholes and may be leaving just as results are taking a turn for the worse, when normal accounting adjustments can't help the firm match investor expectations. Or perhaps the CEO was indeed a genius, whereas the new executive will need time to step into those big shoes.

Many stocks struggle after a star CEO exits. Consider Arthur Blank, who left The Home Depot in 2001; Sandy Weill, who left

Citigroup in 2006; and Jack Welch, who left General Electric Company in 2001. All three led tremendous stock performances, left after receiving universal acclaim, and found that company stock underperformed after their departures.

You Can't Shrink to Greatness

Wall Street typically cheers when a company announces layoffs. Layoffs reduce short-term expenses without substantially affecting revenue. It can make sense from a business perspective: if business contracts, you need fewer people.

A company that lays off workers, however, is admitting that the good times are over, at least at present. Hiring new people costs money in recruitment and training; it takes time for an employee to become competent and fully productive. Reluctantly laying off productive people is management's admission that hard times are here to stay.

As with many indicators, investors can find opportunities by asking whether market perception matches reality. If a company is in widely recognized distress, a layoff can boost the stock price. It suggests that *management* was late to understand the depth of their problems.

In other layoffs, by contrast, the company acknowledges hardships that the *market* has not fully recognized.

For years, it has seemed that the world is running out of oil. There was very little spare capacity, and every new discovery was met with increasing demand and a fall-off in production from current oil fields. In 2008, oil went from $70 to $147 and back to $40 a barrel, an astounding twelve-month change. Traders debated the reasons for price volatility, but largely agreed on the underlying fundamentals of permanently tight supply. Oil companies committed capital to find and develop new sources.

Oil companies had a long stretch of break-even results in the 1980s and 1990s, which starved the industry of young oil engineers. Graduates had flocked to other fields. The industry found itself with an older workforce that would be difficult to replace.

In January 2009, slumping oil prices gave oil companies indifferent returns. Some companies delayed projects. Schlumberger (SLB), the preeminent global firm supplying engineering and oil development support, saw their price decline by 50 percent during the final four months of 2008. Investors debated. Was this just a bull market sell-off, or were lower oil prices here to stay for a while?

Schlumberger signaled its opinion by laying off 1,000 American workers (about 5 percent of its workforce) and a similar portion of its 65,000 overseas staff—all people it would find expensive to replace. The news should have pushed oil bulls to reexamine their assumptions.

Help Wanted

Investors can also find clues among firms and industries that are aggressively hiring. For many years, Google was known as *the* destination for the best young programmers. Google signaled confidence in its future; the best and brightest anointed the company as the ascendant technology leader and drove its considerable revenues and profits.

During the July 2008 conference call, analysts asked why the company's hiring rate had slowed substantially. "I think what you'll see going forward is prudent management of headcount growth.... We are paying a lot of attention to headcount," responded Google CEO Eric Schmidt. It was a subtle warning that the company needed to get expenses under control and that Google's rapid growth phase had ended. The stock had already moved off its November 2007 peak of $732, so perhaps the market had already factored in a slowdown. Nevertheless, the stock sank nearly 50 percent over the next six months as the Google growth machine sputtered, along with the general economy.

Traders can also draw insight by watching where a company plans to hire or cut back, because these moves can signal that the firm expects leading or lagging business opportunities in particular business sectors or geographical areas. An increase in Chinese market hiring, for instance, suggests a growing segment, while a layoff in Brazil could serve as an early warning for a company that traditionally draws good earnings from the region.

Every month, the U.S. government reports employment growth and contraction. In late 2008, as the economy slowed, the report showed health care and education as leaders in hiring—perhaps another clue for alert investors.

Fighting with Short Sellers

It's difficult to appreciate someone who roots against the home team. Companies aren't typically pleased with short sellers, particularly with those who draw attention to a firm's shortcomings. It's hard for executives to spend most of their waking hours trying to build a business, only to hear someone else try to shoot it down—and profit from doing so.

It's one thing to respond to a short seller's thesis with a reasonable, fact-based rebuttal, but it's another to threaten lawsuits or hire a private investigator to trail short sellers or tap their phone lines. Such extreme reactions suggest that a company has something to hide.

In February 2006, Canadian drug company Biovail (BVF) sued Gradient Analytics, an independent research firm specializing in forensic accounting. Gradient had issued a report criticizing Biovail. Biovail also sued a few of Gradient's client hedge funds, which had taken short positions on Biovail.

As the case wound through the courts, the numbers began telling the real story. The stock declined nearly 50 percent in the two years after Biovail filed suit. In March 2008, the SEC sued Biovail and members of its former management team, saying that "present and former senior Biovail executives, obsessed with meeting quarterly and annual earnings guidance, repeatedly overstated earnings and hid losses in order to deceive investors and create the appearance of achieving earnings goals. When it ultimately became impossible to continue concealing the company's inability to meet its own earnings guidance, Biovail actively misled investors and analysts about the reasons for the company's poor performance." Biovail settled the suit for $10 million.

John Mackey, founder and CEO of Whole Foods (WFMI), may also have cared a bit too much about company detractors. On February 21, 2007, Mackey succeeded in his bid to consolidate a major portion of the organic-grocery business by merging with competitor Wild Oats (OATS). People skeptical of Whole Foods' business model and valuation, including short sellers, questioned whether the firm had paid too much and might face antitrust resistance from the government. They were also concerned that Wal-Mart and general supermarkets were offering a greater assortment of organic foods. Mackey had a full plate, needing to complete the acquisition, fully integrate operations, and hold off the competition.

Yet he found time to post on the Yahoo! message board under the moniker "Rahodeb"—an anagram of Deborah, his wife's name—anonymously attacking the doubters and suggesting that Whole Foods was a great investment. His postings came to light during Federal Trade Commission due diligence on the Wild Oats transaction. They found that Mackey had posted more than eleven hundred times between 1999 and 2006.

One might expect contrition, but Mackey defended his actions and again lashed out at skeptics. When the *Wall Street Journal* wrote about the postings on July 12, 2007, the stock price was at $39.50, down from its all-time high of $52.11, a level it reached on the day the company announced the Wild Oats deal. The deal was completed in August. One year later, the company was faced with integrating Wild Oats, a weak balance sheet from rapid expansion, competitive organic offerings at other grocery stores, and a slowing economy. The stock was at $18.25.

Howard Shultz, founder and CEO of Starbucks, also faced skeptics. Short sellers swarmed to the stock in its early growth years, many doubting that customers would pay $2.00 for a cup of coffee they could brew at home for less than twenty cents.

But Shultz handled the doubters with calm, evenhanded professionalism. In a column dated December 13, 2004, Herb Greenberg, an early skeptic, named Shultz his "chief executive of the decade." Greenberg called questioning the company "my biggest single mistake," adding that Starbucks "took all of my calls and answered all of my questions, even though what I wrote was usually critical.... Unlike CEOs who challenge the naysayers, and even attack them, Shultz appeared to begrudgingly respect them." The stock rose nearly twentyfold between 1994 and 2004, during the company's prolific growth phase.

Homes and Skyscrapers

Most chief executive officers earn their pay. They work almost constantly to chart a company's course, motivate employees, and meet with suppliers and customers to ensure that everything runs smoothly. If something goes wrong, shareholders blame the CEO, regardless of who is at fault.

There's nothing wrong with a CEO's desire for a big house. All the same, many executives purchase lavish homes when they feel they've succeeded in business. That achievement, though a good thing in itself, may make them less hungry for future business coups.

In October 2007, Crocker Liu (Arizona State) and David Yermack (New York University) released their academic paper "Where are the Shareholders' Mansions? CEOs' Home Purchases, Stock Sales, and Subsequent Company Performance." They concluded, "we interpret large home acquisitions as signals of CEO entrenchment," and said that "future company performance deteriorates when CEOs acquire extremely large or costly mansions and estates." The professors located the homes of 488 S&P 500 company CEOs. The average house had 6,145 square feet, twelve rooms, more than five acres of land, and a value of $3.1 million. One hundred sixty-four of the CEOs had recently bought new homes, and these were even more impressive, boasting an average 6,635 square feet, thirteen rooms, six acres, and a value of $3.9 million.

The study showed that, the larger the CEO's house, the worse the company's stock performance. Shares of companies whose CEOs lived in above-average homes underperformed shares of companies whose CEOs lived in below-average executive homes. The 2005 difference was 3.35 percent. Companies whose CEOs bought new homes after becoming CEO had stocks that underperformed the S&P 500 by 1.25 per month.

Services such as Google Earth can give an aerial view of any property; Zillow.com can give a property's dimensions and market value estimate. If a company's CEO has a model estate, maybe that executive has forgotten the long hours and hard work that leading a large organization requires.

But there's an exception to every rule. After building Microsoft into an industry giant, Bill Gates planned a state-of-the-art, 66,000-square-foot house in late 1990. By the time he moved into the house in 1997, Microsoft stock was up 1,600 percent. Gates's work ethic never faltered.

Party Time

Other kinds of excess can also signal that company, sector, or industry has peaked. Consider Stephen Schwarzman at private equity titan Blackstone, which uses debt financing to buy underperforming public companies, turn them around, and either sell or take the firms public a few years later. The firm has a long history of outstanding returns, driven in part by Schwarzman's legendary work ethic.

Private equity managers generally espouse the virtues of running a company privately, away from the quarterly performance pressures and additional regulatory costs facing management at a publicly traded company. Nevertheless, Blackstone went public in 2007. Executives were well compensated for the additional hassle. Schwarzman himself sold a portion of his company holdings, receiving $684 million at the IPO price of $31 per share. His total Blackstone holdings were worth $8.83 billion after the first day of trading.

Before the offering, Schwarzman threw himself a sixtieth birthday party and invited hundreds. Rock star Rod Stewart played. The party reportedly cost $3 million and made the front page of many papers. Even then, Reuters ran a story titled "Blackstone CEO Gala Sign of Buyout Boom."

> For some, the party brought back memories of past high times on Wall Street, like the junk bond frenzy led by Michael Milken in the 1980s and the Internet boom in the late 1990s. For others, it was a sign that a buyout bust could be just around the corner.
> "It's the kind of stuff that makes us think that we're at the top," said an executive at another large private equity firm, who did not attend the party.

As often occurs, the signs were hiding in plain sight. The stock (BX) hit $35 the day of the IPO. That marked the stock's top—and the beginning of the end for private equity's acquisition binge. One year later, Blackstone stock was at $18. By the end of 2008, the stock had sunk to $6.50 per share.

Tyco's then-CEO Dennis Kozlowski threw a different but also lavish party, this time on a Roman theme, for his then-wife in June 2001. Tyco picked up half the $2 million tab. That's not a lot of money for a multibillion-dollar firm, but it was indicative of Kozlowski's executive spending habits, and a precursor to charges of fraud and gross mismanagement. On September 19, 2005, Kozlowski was sentenced to eight to twenty-five years for misappropriation of corporate funds and other charges. Karen Kozlowski filed for divorce on July 31, 2006.

These are extreme examples of executive ego and overspending, but such tendencies can also reveal themselves in smaller ways. Notice a company's parking lot. Are the spaces nearest the door reserved for upper management, or for visitors and customers? Does the lobby contain a display showing the real-time price of the company's stock? (A company shouldn't measure itself by daily stock movements alone.) Is the CEO's office enormous and far from every one else? A CEO sets the company's tone, and small matters can send an important signal.

Building Castles in the Sky

Overentitlement can afflict entire countries. Skyscrapers, for example, take a long time to plan and build. A government that plans one must be awfully confident of both the future and the project's financing.

That was the case in Kuala Lumpur, which broke ground on the Petronas Towers in 1992, when Asia was very popular with investors. The project was completed in 1998, a year after the Asian currency crisis.

Super-structures often foreshadow economic panic. The Sears Tower in Chicago and World Trade Center in New York broke ground in 1973, just as the United States was entering a nasty recession. The Chrysler Building (1928) and Empire State Building (1930) started just before the Great Depression. Russia stopped construction on what was to be Europe's tallest building in the fall of 2008, when the country's once booming economy came to a shuttering halt.

Stadium Naming Rights: The Winner's Curse

In any auction, it's easy to get caught up in the bidding and forget an item's intrinsic value. That leads to the winner's curse: you won, but you paid too high a price.

The winner's curse often afflicts companies that win auctions for the right to name sports stadiums. There is some marketing value in having the company's name on the building and tickets. All too often, however, companies overpay for the privilege.

Enron paid $100 million to name Houston's Enron Field when the Astros got their new stadium in April 1999. It was renamed Minute Maid Park three years later, when Enron entered bankruptcy court. CMGI paid $114 million in a fifteen-year deal to name CMGI Field for the New England Patriots, on a day that the stock traded at more than $43. CMGI announced bankruptcy two years later, when the stock traded at 40 cents. In 2006, Citigroup agreed to pay $20 million per year for 20 years to name Citi Field a new home for the New York Mets. Two years later, Citigroup accepted a government bailout package to help them absorb $306 billion in risky assets. The stock was at $5.

Jumping the Shark

Every television show has a natural life span. When a show goes beyond that point, characters become stale, and writers exhaust their best ideas. The writers grasp at straws and introduce plots that don't make sense. In the best-known example, *Happy Days*' Fonzie jumps a shark pen on water skis while wearing his trademark leather jacket. The episode gave rise to the term *jump the shark*, referring to an enterprise whose best ideas are behind it.

Corporations can be said to have jumped the shark when they pursue an acquisition that doesn't make sense. Consider the following:

- Old-line media titan Time Warner bought America Online (AOL) in January 2000 for more than $180 billion in a "merger of equals" near the top of the Internet craze. Time Warner said it was looking for "media convergence."
- Online auctioneer eBay bought start-up Internet phone service Skype for $2.6 billion in September 2005. At the time, Skype had $7 million in revenues and no profits. EBay claimed the deal would help auction customers better interact.
- Coca-Cola bought Columbia Pictures in 1982 for $700 million in cash and stock, part of a diversification effort. Coca-Cola divested Columbia in a spin-off in 1987, as investors had become tired of the unit's uneven business results. (Columbia's widely panned, very expensive movie *Ishtar* was the final straw for many.)

Mergers and acquisitions should be about product extensions, distribution channels, and lower costs. Ideally, deals should involve a clear buyer and seller—it's difficult to manage a merger of equals. When a deal doesn't make intuitive sense, watch out.

A Profitable Shoe Shine

There's a classic story that in the summer of 1929, überinvestor Joe Kennedy was getting nervous about the stock market. The economy was in great shape, but it seemed that valuations were getting stretched. Back then, the market was an enclave of the rich. There were no 401(k) funds introducing the masses to the market's daily vicissitudes.

With these concerns running through his mind, Kennedy went to get his shoes shined. The shoe boy recognized him. In normal times, the boy may have talked about the weather or the Yankees. Recognizing Kennedy, the shoe boy explained how well he was doing in the market and tried to tell Kennedy about a stock he thought Kennedy should buy.

If the local shoe boy was in the market, Kennedy realized, there weren't many buyers left. The shoeshine boy confirmed Kennedy's own sense that the market was extremely vulnerable to a broad sell-off. Kennedy sold holdings and missed the crash that arrived a few months later.

Sometimes, though not often, an everyday event suggests that a trend just can't last. Between 2002 and 2005, prospective buyers rushed to buy real estate in California, Las Vegas, Phoenix, Florida, and many other spots around the country. Banks offered housing loans to borrowers without requiring documentation of the applicant's ability to pay. Even *Playboy*'s Miss May 2005 said that she hoped to have a successful career in real estate.

It took a while, but the long period of excess began to unwind in 2007. A wave of foreclosures followed, sparking a deep recession that began in 2008 and spread into 2009.

RESOURCES

Michelle Leder looks at interesting SEC filings and other little noticed disclosures at www.footnoted.org.

Enron is a rich source of cautionary tales of corporate malfeasance. Two books to consider are *Conspiracy of Fools* by Kurt Eichenwald and *The Smartest Guys in the Room* by Bethany McLean and Peter Elkind.

The U.S. government report on employment growth, among many other labor statistics, is on the U.S. Bureau of Labor Statistics (BLS) Web site (www.bls.gov).

Part III

Following the Smart Money

Our best thoughts come from others.

—RALPH WALDO EMERSON

THE PLEASURE OF A new idea or original insight is one of the best parts of an investor's job. But though it's fun—and potentially profitable—to generate novel ways of considering the market, it's also wise to look at what other investors are doing. Traders who follow and understand moves made by other market participants effectively stand on those investors' shoulders, gaining a better overall view of the market.

The upcoming chapters examine how to track the market's movers and shakers: company executives who see business unfold before them daily; big money working in the futures market; the really big money working in the credit markets; the money that flows through IPOs, mergers, and buybacks; and the gurus and superstar investors with great instincts and deep research staffs. We'll talk about why they do the things they do, discuss their blind spots and limitations, and examine the insights retail investors can gain from them.

Chapter **11**

The Insiders

All animals are equal, but some animals are more equal than others.
—GEORGE ORWELL, in *Animal Farm*

As I grow older, I pay less attention to what men say. I just watch what they do.
—ANDREW CARNEGIE, the world's richest man of his time

THEY MAY OR may not be good investors, but the people who run a company certainly have a better view of its future than the rest of us do. These stewards of capital may not be fortune-tellers, but the fog of uncertainty that surrounds a company's future is a little thinner for them.

As long as there have been markets, traders have taken advantage of insider knowledge. In the market's early days, most members of the public didn't buy stock. They felt the game was rigged, dominated by a few elite participants who used their superior access to information to swindle the masses. The problem came to a head after the 1929 stock market crash, when the public had become heavily invested in the market and had lost much of its savings. Reports of backroom deals surfaced, suggesting that corporate leaders and their associates used insider information to line their pockets.

The Securities and Exchange Commission (SEC) formed in 1934 as a response to the crash and the unfair advantages that insiders held. It became illegal to buy or sell securities based on "material and nonpublic" information. Over the last seventy-five years there has been debate over what "material" and "nonpublic" means from a legal perspective, but the general principle—the importance of a level playing field—has held firm. A healthy economy works best with a vibrant market, which is only possible with broad participation. Insider-trading rules help encourage broad participation by making most information equally available to all investors.

This chapter will review current insider-trading rules, discuss what information investors can glean from insider trades of individual securities, and finish with a look at how combining insider activity data can give useful views of individual sectors or the overall market.

Updated Insider Rules

As discussed in Chapter 8, management once commonly updated Wall Street through conversations with favored analysts. In the 1990s, for instance, Morgan Stanley analyst Jack Grubman had the ear of leading figures in the telecommunication industry. Grubman acted as a bridge between investment bankers, who were doing deals, and management, who decided who received the underlying business. His position gave Grubman unusual access and industry insight, but cost him some independence and objectivity. He was under immense pressure to make all the news look good, and didn't allow himself enough space to see valuations and industry developments with a skeptical eye.

In the wake of the corporate scandals of 2001 and 2002, with Jack Grubman as a poster boy for compromised analysts, the SEC passed Regulation Fair Disclosure (Reg FD). This rule forced management to reveal corporate developments only in settings where the general public could hear the news at the same time that analysts heard it. On balance, the rule has helped even the playing field for small investors.

But Reg FD does not stand for "full disclosure." Management can say nothing and be within the rule's guidelines. In fact, saying very little can be the safest and surest way for management to avoid accidentally revealing material information in a nonpublic setting.

The SEC rewrote rules affecting corporate governance in 2002, alongside the passage of the Sarbanes-Oxley Act (SOX). The new guidelines update corporate reporting rules and require insiders to report transactions within two business days, instead of the tenth day of the following month, as the previous rules required.

The SEC strictly enforces the rules governing the purchase and sale of securities by executives who can potentially profit from material, inside information. Familiarity with these rules can help traders better understand the value and limitations of insider moves.

The rules are complex. Broadly, they state that

- The SEC identifies insiders as company directors, officials (CEO, CFO, etc.), or any individual with more than a 10 percent stake in the company.
- An insider cannot tip off someone else regarding a company development. If the tipster acts on this information, the insider can be found guilty of and liable for insider trading.
- Insiders may not buy and then sell company stock within a six-month time frame for short-swing profits. Consequently, insiders tend to buy stock when they feel the company will do well over the *long* term.
- Insiders must electronically document their trades, using what's known as a Form 4. Firms annually file a list of directors and officers, noting the company share interest of each, using a Form 14a.
- Insiders are subject to additional restrictions if they have significant material information. Executives aware of or negotiating a merger agreement, for instance, cannot make trades based on that information.
- Insiders can avoid mistakenly violating these rules by implementing a general investment plan at a time when they are not in possession of insider information. These are called 10b5-1 plans and will be discussed later in this chapter.

Academic Review

In their study "How Informative Are Analyst Recommendations and Insider Trades?" three professors (Jim Hsieh from George Mason University, Lilian K. Ng of the University of Wisconsin at Milwaukee, and Qinghai Wang of the Georgia Institute of Technology) analyzed the interactions between analyst recommendations and insider trading, and the investment value of each. They considered 1994 through 2003, noting quarters in which the consensus analyst ranking had gone up or down. Then they looked for net purchases or sales among the company's insiders. Among other findings are the following:

- Insider buys are informative and have better return predictability than analyst recommendations. When insiders were bullish, their stocks tended to outperform the market, regardless of what analysts said.
- When insiders sold and analysts issued downgrades, stocks tended to lag the market over the next four quarters.
- When insiders were quiet (no buying or selling) and analysts downgraded expectations, stocks did even worse than when insiders sold concurrently with analyst downgrades.

This last point suggests that insiders don't know when to sell. The researchers, however, argue that regulations governing insider actions may preclude insiders from acting on bearish information. In this case, "downgrades help convey such negative information to the market," the researchers said.

The study's time period overlapped Reg FD's introduction. Researchers found that their conclusions were even more pronounced after the more stringent reporting rules went into effect in October 2000.

Executive Buying

With most executives already motivated to increase company value, there is only one reason for them to take their own money and buy the company's stock in the open market: they think the market price is too low and that the market underappreciates their business prospects. Logical enough—but remember that not all insider buying is created equal. When looking at purchases, it's important to consider:

WHO IS BUYING

The executives closest to a company's day-to-day operations offer the best insight into firm performance. C-level (CEO, CFO, COO, etc.) executives tend to have sharp business minds and a deep, broad view of the company. Board of directors members and other high level employees, such as vice presidents, also have a better view of the future than an outside investor.

The chief financial officer (CFO) typically has the best seat in the house. Traditionally the numbers person, the CFO usually understands what and who is moving company stock. This executive should know what key stockholders expect from revenue or earnings, as well as whether the company is on track to meet or exceed those expectations. The CFO also deals with the accounting staff and knows how aggressively or conservatively they are reporting the numbers. In broad terms, CFOs are measured and circumspect, tending to look first for potential problems. In many firms, the CFO is "Dr. No," the hardheaded realist who decides which major initiatives deserve company capital.

If the CFO is buying, that's an especially good sign. And if the CEO and others are buying but the CFO is conspicuous by his absence, it's probably worth the time to find out why.

Pay attention, too, when previously successful insiders—those with a history of well-timed sales and purchases—are trading. Some executives have a knack for timing purchases and sales. Directors sitting on many boards may be outstanding investors in their own right and legitimately use their inside views to presciently position a portfolio. Perhaps a certain executive has been with the company or in the industry for a long time and has a history of good buying decisions. If that person has recently bought or sold stock, chances are good that he or she will be right again.

Several services track insider trades. A few free services automatically collect trading information filed with the SEC www.sec.gov/edgar.shtml and put a few filters in place. These free services include Sec Form 4 (www.secform4.com), J3 Services Group (www.j3sg.com), and Insider Monitor (www.insider-monitor.com). Note the codes that differentiate activity, such as an open market purchase or an option exercise. These services pick up these codes, but a look at the source filing can help investors more fully understand and analyze the insider activity.

Yahoo! Finance offers a nice history of insider activity, arranged by company, that can help spot insiders with strong track records. For online subscribers, *Barron's* offers a section highlighting notable insider activity (http://online.barrons.com/article/13d_filings.html).

Many institutional services do extensive research on inside activity for their clients. They sift through filings and check their databases for individuals who have made particularly canny trades in the past. These services also aggregate information across sectors and the broad market, using that data to notice potential signals and their relative strengths. (It can be particularly bullish, for example, if executives across the semiconductor industry are all buying stock at historically aggressive levels for that sector.) These paid services include InsiderScore (www.insiderscore. com), Vickers Weekly Insider Report (www.vickers-stock.com), InsiderInsights (www.insiderinsights.com), and Muzea Insider Consulting Services (www.smartinsider.net). Many of these firms' executives talk to the financial press on occasion. Get their free insights by setting a Google Alert for George Muzea (Muzea Research), Jonathan Moreland (InsiderInsights), or Ben Silverman (InsiderScore).

Conviction

Market participants take note when executives tell a conference-call audience that they believe their stock is undervalued, or when a well-compensated officer buys a few thousand dollars worth of stock. But it's a mark of conviction when an insider buys a significant amount of stock. No single dollar amount shows that conviction. A billionaire sitting on the board of directors might spend $1 million, a relatively small sum for that investor, and one that doesn't necessarily show a high level of enthusiasm. A vice president with a net worth of $1 million, on the other hand, can show a great level of conviction by spending $200,000.

It's best to review trades and holdings on a case-by-case basis. A long-time executive might own 5,000 shares, for example, purchased years ago. By purchasing another 5,000 shares the executive doubles that position, possibly at a significant time for the firm. A larger position accumulated over many years of small, regular, monthly purchases would not have the same signal significance.

The executive's background matters, too. Yahoo! Finance tracks job descriptions and salaries of many executives. Perhaps the executive in the first example above, who suddenly purchases another 5,000 shares after a long period of inactivity, makes $150,000 per year and is chief of research and development. This case, of a division head in charge of developing new products suddenly spending nearly a year's after-tax salary to double stock holdings, would be a more significant potential signal than a billionaire director spending $1 million to increase stock holdings by five percent.

Safety in Numbers

Is a particular company's stock a great value? A pattern of several insiders purchasing stock suggests that it is, particularly if those insiders are C-level executives and/or the group includes the company CFO. Just one insider buyer, however, is a weaker signal.

Volume matters, too. A firm's executives might collectively buy relatively small amounts of stock—a few thousand dollars' worth, or less than a few percent of their annual compensation—to give investors, employees, customers, and suppliers the impression that management strongly believes in the company's future. An attempt to send this positive signal with a minimal cash outlay should be seen more as marketing than as an attempt to gain from the market's misunderstanding of the company's intrinsic value.

Buying into Strength

Insiders tend to buy and hold. The SEC requires that they hold stock for at least six months; they also want to avoid the impression that they are "flipping" their own firm's stock. They often buy on weakness, when they feel the market has pushed the stock too low. It's especially interesting, therefore, when executives pay *up* for a stock.

Software company Opsware (OPSW), for example, traded around $4.50 per share in the summer of 2005. There was one insider buy during the summer, but executive purchases began in earnest in late 2005, with a series of management purchases between $5.50 and $6.50 per share. The stock price didn't return to its lower levels, staying above $6.50 until July 2007, when Hewlett-Packard bought the firm at $14.25 per share.

Meaningless Buys

Some purchases don't mean as much. Many investors ignore

- Purchases made by a new employee. Many companies require that executives buy a certain amount of stock on the open market within the first year of hiring, spending perhaps six months' salary. Many times, the company itself extends a low- or no-interest loan to finance the purchase. This is not a conviction-based buy.

- Buying within a company's ESOP (Employee Stock Ownership Plan). Many ESOPs offer stock to employees at a discount to the market price. These are usually small purchases.
- Purchases as part of an IPO. Some companies require officers to buy stock as part of an IPO. Again, this is not conviction-based buying, and doesn't help predict successful IPOs. It is potentially significant, though, if executives buy stock on the open market *after* an initial public offering is complete.

Insider Selling

With the increased importance of options in an executive's total compensation, selling stock can be seen as a form of delayed payment. An executive may have many reasons to sell: to pay for a wedding, buy a house, or diversify holdings on the advice of a financial adviser. Sales are generally a weaker signal than are buys.

Sometimes selling can actually be bullish. An executive whose options are about to expire may exercise the options, selling just enough to cover taxes. The executive reports a sale, but has actually shown confidence in the stock's value by keeping a majority of the option grant shares.

A lack of selling can also be bullish, as well as an absence of selling into a nice advance can be tacit approval by insiders. Executives normally sell a portion of their holdings over time, to generate cash and guard against the possibility that the stock's value will drop. A lack of executive selling in a firm with good stock performance may signal that the people running the company have a higher than normal conviction that the stock will continue to advance.

Investors should worry, though, when insiders sell a large amount of stock—in absolute dollar terms, or as a percentage of holdings—in a short period of time. In June 2005, at the height of the housing boom, Toll Brothers (TOL) was building and delivering high-end homes at a historic rate, and had become a stock market darling. Toll traded at $5 per share (split-adjusted) in March 2000, at the height of the Internet-fueled Nasdaq boom. Only deep-value investors wanted the shares. Subsequent deep interest-rate cuts and favorable tax policies fueled a rapid increase in home values and home building. By March 2005, the stock traded near $40, with the company on track to earn $4.78 per share that year, up 90 percent from 2004.

In February 2005, Toll CEO Robert Toll sold $110 million of stock and followed with $134 million more, unloaded in four July sales. He hadn't sold stock in nine years. Elsewhere in the industry, other CEOs were also unloading stock: Bruce Karatz of KB Home (KBH) sold $76 million in company stock in July, and Chad Dreier of Ryland (RYL) collected more than $38 million in a string of sales during 2005 and 2006. All still held substantial holdings, but the sales should have given investors pause. Toll Brothers stock crested at $58.25 on July 22, 2005 before starting its decline to $24.75, where it landed two years later.

Selling into Weakness

Selling into weakness is another warning signal. When insiders sell stock at decreasing prices, it's a sign that they think company prospects are deteriorating faster than the market recognizes. The stock is richly valued, they believe, even at the lesser price. Again, this sign is strongest when several insiders show the same pattern, and when insiders are selling large amounts in either nominal or percentage terms.

Actions, it's said, speak louder than words, and it's often instructive to track differences between executive statements and executive trades. Angelo Mozilo, founder and then-CEO of Countrywide Bank (CFC), is one example. Countrywide was a market leader in underwriting mortgage loans during the housing boom. Countrywide reported record profits, and the stock rose from $12 in early 2003 to more than $40 in early 2007. As the bloom started to come off the mortgage lending business, skeptics questioned whether Countrywide could handle looming defaults from loans written in prior years. Mozilo was adamant in defense of the firm's underwriting standards and ability to weather write-offs.

His stock sales told a different story. Between November 2006 and August 2007, Mozilo pocketed $138 million from stock sales, even as the company used its own capital to buy back stock in late 2006, at nearly $40 per share. Faced with rising foreclosure rates and a deteriorating balance sheet, Countrywide was forced to raise capital; Bank of America (BAC) bought $2 billion in CFC preferred stock in August 2007, when common stock traded at $22 per share. At the time, many smart, well-known value investors thought the market was radically undervaluing Countrywide's stock. But they would have been well served by pondering why Mozilo was aggressively selling his stock. As conditions worsened, Mozilo was forced to sell Countrywide to Bank of America, which offered 0.2 shares of Bank of America for every one share of Countrywide, or about $4.00 per Countrywide share when the deal closed in July 2008.

10b5-1 Plans

To help executives navigate complex insider-trading rules, the SEC lets insiders make a written plan for mechanically buying or selling stock. The insider must create the plan at a time when he or she does not have material inside information.

Once written, the plan goes on autopilot, staying outside the insider's direct control. An executive who wants to sell 50,000 shares might plan to sell 1,000 shares every Monday, for example, at a price no lower than $50 per share. This type of plan provides a legal safe harbor, protecting the executive from accusations of insider trading. Insiders have only to prove that they had no special information at the time they initiated the plan.

Surprisingly, executives are not required to disclose the existence or details of 10b5-1 plans. As a matter of good corporate governance, however, many firms do require executives to file these important corporate developments. If the information is publicly available, it is as a footnote on Form 4.

Researchers have found that the mere initiation of a 10b5-1 plan is a more bearish indicator than are other types of insider selling. In a December 2006 paper titled "Do Insiders Trade Strategically within the SEC Rule 10b5-1 Safe Harbor?" Stanford Professor Alan Jagolinzer analyzed 10b5-1 trading patterns. He found that these sales outperformed outsider trades by 5.9 percent over the following six months, and that executives tended to sell *after* good news and *before* bad news. The paper's summary notes that "there is evidence that participants' sales, on average, generate abnormal trade returns, that a substantive proportion of selected 10b5-1 plan initiations are associated with pending adverse news disclosure, and that participants terminate sales plans before positive shifts in firm returns."

Follow-up research from Gradient Analytics, an independent market research company, determined that trading plans led to even greater underperformance. Gradient deems plans "aggressive" when they last less than twelve months and/or sell more than 50 percent of holdings.

Both research projects suggest that executives take advantage of legal protections, particularly when their plans are both aggressive and short term. They have great flexibility to start, stop, and amend plans as they see fit. Wise investors pay attention when executives start or stop plans, or when an executive runs multiple plans, seemingly for strategic purposes.

In a December 2006 article, *BusinessWeek* recounted the selling plan created by Broadcom (BRCM) CEO Scott McGregor. McGregor had a plan that averaged sales of 2,750 shares per month (netting about $110,000) from May 2005 to December 2005. Between January 3 and March 2, 2006, he quickened the pace dramatically, selling 350,000 shares for a net $19 million. The stock had surged towards $46 per share when the company announced strong earnings on January 27, 2006. The 10b5-1 plan sold into that price strength. One year later, the stock was at $31.

Aggregating the Data

Company executives can signal future direction; so, too, can insiders at other companies in that industry. In summer 2005, executives across the housing industry were selling stock, adding significance to Robert Toll's large sales. And in spring 2003, when insiders were buying large amounts of stock in the beaten-up technology sector, it helped support a bullish thesis for the group.

Professional services can provide tools that help paint a picture of a sector or a market. Each sector has its own historical patterns. For instance, technology employees get a comparatively large amount of compensation in the form of option grants, so they naturally sell options more frequently than do utility executives. **FIGURE 11.1** shows the overall market buy/sell ratio for company insiders from 2004 to 2008. Buying activity spikes signals that insiders generally saw value, as they did in November 2008.

As a group, insiders tend to be too early, and their buying tends to be more telling than their aggregate selling. The spikes up (heavy insider selling) were most pronounced in late 2004 and late 2006. Rather than serve as an immediate sell signal, they better served as a warning of storm clouds on the horizon.

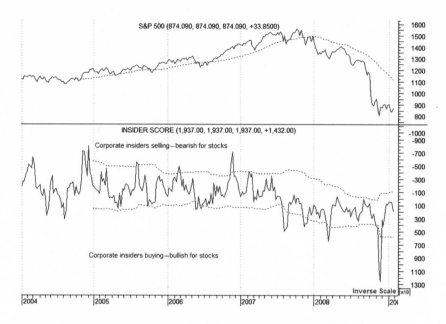

Figure 11.1   InsiderScore aggregate buy/sell ratio, 2004–2008

Source: InsiderScore.com

Buying, however, tends to be a good barometer of stock levels when executives believe the market provides good value. Spikes down (heavy insider buying) corresponded with sharp market sell-offs and confirmed that selling was likely overdone, based on current fundamentals.

RESOURCES

A good review of insider trading laws is available at http://www.insider-monitor. com/articles/insider-trading-law-usa.html.

Free services tracking insider trading include: www.secform4.com, www.j3sg.com, and www.insider-monitor.com.

Paid services tracking and commenting on insider activity include: www. insiderscore.com, www.vickers-stock.com, www.insiderinsights.com, and www. smartinsider.net.

Books outlining the case for following insiders include George Muzea's *The Vital Few vs. the Trivial Many: Invest with the Insiders, Not the Masses*, Jonathan Moreland's *Profit from Legal Insider Trading*, and H. Nejat Seyhun's *Investment Intelligence from Insider Trading*.

Chapter 12

Looking to the Futures

Selling a soybean contract short is worth two years at the Harvard Business School.

—ROBERT STOVALL, Wood Asset Management

THE TYPICAL PERSON on the street had never heard of the U.S. Commodity Futures Trading Commission (CFTC)—at least, not until the summer of 2008. Oil experienced a superspike that season, one that took retail gasoline to a nosebleed $4 per gallon. Filling a truck could cost more than $100. Car dealerships, the lifeblood of many small towns, went bust as row after row of SUVs stood unwanted at any price. General Motors, Ford, and Chrysler hemorrhaged even more money than usual.

The weakening dollar and increasing difficulty in meeting the global thirst for oil may have explained the gradual increase to $100 per barrel (equivalent to $3.50 for a gallon of gasoline), it didn't satisfy the public's search for a reason that oil had gone from $100 to more than $147 a barrel in just a few months. Congress wanted answers; to get them it turned to the CFTC, which regulates the futures market.

A future is an *obligation* to pay and take delivery of an asset, usually a commodity such as corn or gold, at a given future date. The person selling, or shorting a contract, locks in a price for the asset and is obligated to deliver the asset at the given future date. Equity investors can use the forward-looking futures market to better forecast earnings for companies that deal with commodities. By charting moves in financial futures, traders may see signals that can help verify or contradict other indicators.

Futures contracts trade around the world, notably on the New York Mercantile Exchange (NYMEX) and the Chicago Mercantile Exchange (CME). Futures contracts rarely end in actual delivery; instead the contracts are closed just before expiration, and the parties exchange cash instead. Both parties "roll forward" their contracts, settling current contracts and maintaining exposure by establishing new futures contracts.

By its nature, a futures contract is a leveraged vehicle. A stock investor can employ a maximum leverage of 2:1: a trader who owns $100,000 in marginable securities can get a loan from a broker for another $100,000. A futures position, on the other hand, requires a much lower cash percentage. For instance, a trader expecting a rise in the S&P 500 could put up $25,000 as an initial margin deposit (which would vary with market volatility) to buy one S&P 500 contract. That contract is worth 250 times the starting index level, so a futures contract with a beginning S&P 500 level of 900 controls $225,000, or 900 × 250 in stock. If the market goes up to 945—a 5 percent increase—the future is then worth $236,250, and the trader makes $11,250, or a 45 percent return on the $25,000 deposit. However, if the market goes *down* 5 percent, the trader loses 45 percent of the deposit and would need to post additional collateral.

Just as the National Association of Securities Dealers (NASD) audits brokerage firms trading stocks, the CFTC oversees futures dealers, and can monitor compliance by checking trading records.

Under CFTC rules, no one person or entity can hold more than a set number of contracts, which varies by commodity. This rule goes back to the infamous Hunt brothers (Nelson Bunker Hunt and William Herbert Hunt were heirs to an oil fortune), who in the early 1970s decided to buy silver as a hedge against inflation. In the fall of 1979, the Hunts teamed with wealthy Arab families to buy up to 200 million ounces of silver, equal to half the world's supply.

Silver was at $2 per ounce when the Hunts started buying, and moved to $5 per ounce in early 1979. By early 1980, silver rocketed to over $50 an ounce, because the Hunts, who controlled much of the available supply, made it hard to buy. New speculators rushed in to buy on the promise of a "new era" for silver.

The government took two actions. First, the CFTC changed the rules for silver by requiring liquidation trading: trading was allowed only to close out existing contracts, not to create new positions.

Second, COMEX, a division of the New York Mercantile Exchange, countered the Hunt's corner on silver by raising the margin requirements. Anyone long a silver future had to put up more capital to maintain the position. The highly leveraged Hunts couldn't meet the margin calls and were forced to sell, collapsing the price of silver. On March 27, 1980 (a day known as "Silver Thursday"), the price fell from $21.62 to $10.80 per ounce. The Hunts declared bankruptcy and their broker, the Bache Group, went out of business.

Transparency also makes it easier to understand what other traders are doing. The CFTC began publishing the number of open futures contracts in 1962, initially mailing a monthly statement. Now the report is available at www.cftc.gov every Friday. It lists open futures positions as of the previous Tuesday, so the data is three days old at its release.

Unlike sentiment surveys, the Commitments of Traders (COT) reports are based on *actual* positions taken by the market's largest traders. These traders must report their positions every day to the CFTC; the public learns of their net efforts every Friday. Mutual funds, by contrast, report their holdings every quarter.

FIGURE 12.1 shows the CFTC's basic report for the S&P futures contract as of September 16, 2008. This report provides:

A) Size of Contract. S&P 500 Index × $250.00 means that every one-point move in the S&P 500 changes the value of the futures

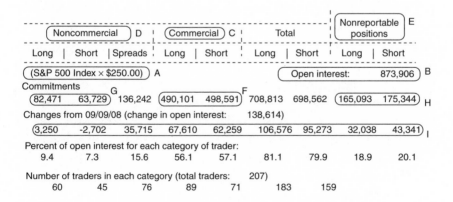

Figure 12.1   COT report for S&P 500 futures as of September 16, 2008

Source: CFTC

contract by $250. A high degree of leverage allows quick market exposure, which makes future contracts attractive to large-scale money managers.

B) Open Interest. When two qualified parties agree to enter a trade, they create a new contract. This data shows the number of contracts currently outstanding. In this case, there are 873,906 contracts outstanding, so more than $218 million is won and lost for every one point the S&P 500 moves.

C) Commercial. These traders use the futures market to hedge their business operations. For instance, General Mills may buy wheat futures to lock in a price for their cereal. A farm cooperative may sell (short) futures to guarantee a price for its upcoming wheat crop. Investment bankers, for their parts, use futures contracts on the S&P 500 and other financial futures to hedge their portfolios.

Every contract is different, but commercial traders tend to sell (short) contracts, because this group is dominated by parties who want to lock in price. There are more farmers, for instance, who want to guarantee a price for part of their crop than there are companies such as General Mills looking to lock in their cost. As a result, commercial traders for wheat (and most commodities) are net sellers. They need net buyers to balance the selling demand.

D) Noncommercial Traders (or Large Traders). These traders have no tangible business in a future's underlying asset. The group, which includes hedge funds and floor traders (called locals), speculate on which way the asset will move. This group provides liquidity for commercial traders, and therefore tends to be buyers, net long. The commission sets the minimum reporting level for large traders, typically at around fifty contracts. To prevent undue control over the market, the CFTC limits these traders to a certain exposure level, which varies by asset class.

E) Nonreportable Positions (or Small Traders). These traders hold fewer than the reportable level and are not required to report their positions to the CFTC. A mixed group, small traders include small commercial hedgers, sophisticated speculators, and some market dabblers. Small traders were often right throughout 2008, despite a reputation for representing the "dumb money."

F) Commercial Position (Long and Short)

G) Noncommercial (Large Trader) Position (Long and Short)

H) Nonreportable (Small Trader) Position (Long and Short). The numbers show the open long and short contracts for each group. Services tracking COT data normally show one net figure. The size of the positions underlying the net total can also be revealing. A net figure of –5,000 could represent a long component of 5,000 and a short component of 10,000, for instance, with smaller blocks forming a potentially less combustible combination. But the same net figure might represent 50,000 long and 55,000 short positions, large blocks that present a potential threat to market stability. A small market move could cause real trouble for a trader.

That may have happened when oil went from $100 to $140 in a matter of weeks. Traders who were short the contract needed to either put up more collateral, in the form of cash or other pledged assets, or exit their position. Those choosing to exit had to "buy in" (or close) their positions, forcing the price even higher. Large traders would have been particularly vulnerable, because they don't have operating capacity to fall back on. Exxon might be a commercial trader, and though the company would be disappointed to lock in a low price, they can still deliver oil to the market.

Opportunistic traders on the sideline may see an imbalance such as this one and purchase contracts, knowing that those with short positions are being forced to buy in their contracts, thereby exacerbating the market's move.

Spread refers to traders who are not taking directional bets. For instance, a trader might be long February natural gas and short April natural gas as a way of betting that the difference—or spread—between the two will contract.

I) Changes in Commitments. This number notes the change in each category from the prior week. Very large changes can signify that a group has newly found conviction. A large decrease from a historically high level of open interest could suggest that something new has happened to compel a change in positioning.

Knowing Where Parties Stand

The world has gotten more complex since the first COT report in 1962. There are many other ways investors gain market exposure, and these methods directly and indirectly affect the futures market.

Even so, the futures market remains the largest arena for matching the buyers and sellers of everything from orange juice to interest rates. It's where traders place their biggest bets. Moves made in the S&P futures pit in Chicago often determine the direction of underlying stock prices trading in New York. In that sense, some believe the tail now wags the dog.

Just as in the equity markets, a trader wanting even more exposure can buy options on predicted futures contract movements. Investors should consider options bets as part of the total picture of trader positions.

Commodity Links to Stocks (and Vice Versa)

Investors can analyze COT data for information on trader positions in financial markets such as the Nasdaq 100, S&P 500, and long-term Treasury bonds. Equity investors can also gather commodity information from the COT. For example, ConocoPhillips's (COP) stock price movement has some connection to price changes for oil, natural gas, and gasoline. Clues gathered from experts on these commodities can lend insight into the future profitability of companies connected to them. Exxon Mobil (XOM), for instance, may have an excellent management team and vertically integrated business model, but the firm will make less money if oil is at $50 a barrel than it will with oil at $100 a barrel. If commodities traders are very bearish, it may be worthwhile to check the underlying fundamentals and consider paring a portfolio's energy exposure.

When a commodity moves sharply, equity markets can signal whether most equity investors think the change is based on fundamentals, or on an out-of-sync futures market. When oil-related stock prices changed little after commodity oil spiked from $100 to $147 a barrel, it suggested that the equities market thought the high price wouldn't last.

Kurt Wulff, an independent researcher, is one analyst who uses the futures market in his energy-sector stock analysis. Read his stock reports (on a two-week delay from paid-subscriber release) at www.mcdep.com.

Swaps and Index Funds

Theoretically, at least, the equity markets place no limits on the number of shares available in a particular company. If investors bid IBM up to $500 per share, IBM could issue millions of new shares to an eager audience, pocketing the cash in return. Large fluctuations in IBM's stock price have little or no direct effect on those who aren't trading it.

That's not so in the commodity markets. There is only so much orange juice concentrate, and a limit to lumber. Even a global market such as oil has a defined physical capacity. Wild fluctuations in commodity prices *do* affect everyday people as they visit the grocery store or gas station. Investment demand and basic commodity-consumption demand are intertwined.

For years, commodity demand dominated the market, with investment demand fairly contained. That has changed in recent years with the greater influence of hedge funds and the broader investment scope of many large pension funds.

The most influential hedge funds operate as large speculators, with size limits on their positions. They have gotten around this limit by buying swaps from investment banks. Swaps and futures contracts operate in essentially the same way, but with a crucial difference: In a swap, the contract is between an investor (such as a hedge fund) and an investment bank. If the investment bank doesn't want to carry the bet, it can go to the futures market and make an offsetting trade. The bank makes money by charging the investor fund a greater commission than it can charge in the futures market.

Banks aren't much involved with commodities—they don't grow corn or make ethanol, for instance—so they're not obvious commercial hedgers. But banks as a group have a hedging exemption from the CFTC, which allows them to trade without fitting the traditionally defined profile of a commercial hedger. As of early 2009, they are not constrained by large-trader position limits, but the futures market as a whole is undergoing review and scrutiny.

The banks have company. Pension funds became increasingly interested in commodities, beginning around 2004, as commodities broadly outperformed equities in 2002 and 2003. Pension funds often base decisions on asset allocation targets; they can be late to recognize an established investment trend. By the time an investment committee decides that an asset class is acceptable, the move has likely mostly played itself out. Pension funds are so large, however, that their entry often serves to extend a trend that would otherwise have run out of steam.

Led by university endowments at such leading institutions as Yale and Harvard, institutional investors also began entering the commodities market in the early 1990s. They sought good returns and vehicles that were not correlated to equities markets, which commodities then offered. Their vehicles of choice were commodity index funds tied to the Goldman Sachs Commodity Index (GSCI), which offer exposure to a broad cross section of the commodities market.

Before pension funds and institutional investors increased their exposure, the futures market enjoyed a balance between the naturally net-short commercial hedgers and the naturally net-long speculators. As pension funds increasingly entered the game, however, long-only index funds pressured commercial hedging and pushed prices higher. **TABLE 12.1** shows GSCI composition as of February 2, 2009.

How to Interpret the Data

There are a variety of ways to consider various trader categories and data. The most common approach is to compare what commercial traders and large speculators are doing. As discussed before, commercial traders arguably have the highest level of knowledge about basic supply and demand and therefore have a well-informed opinion on proper price levels. They tend to buy or cover short hedges when they think a price is too low, and sell or add to hedged positions when they think a price is too high.

Large speculators include hedge funds and traders with shorter time frames. They tend to follow current trends and add to their positions if trends are in their favor. Because of the boom/bust nature of commodity cycles, trends tend to persist in the nonfinancial group of commodities. Traders often push their winning positions, and frequently have their greatest exposure to long-established trends as these top out and start to reverse.

Observers might look for times that large traders are at yearly exposure highs (either long or short) and commercial traders are heading in the other direction. Rather than anticipating a reversal based on this imbalance, it can be practical to wait for the trend to reverse and the gap to begin to narrow. If the trend has been in place long enough—between a few months and a few years, or long enough for investors to grow accustomed to it—the reversal will

Table 12.1 Goldman Sachs Commodity Index composition in percent of dollar weights, February 2, 2009

Energy	63.49	Industrial Metals	6.66	Precious Metals	4.07	Agriculture	19.29	Livestock	6.49
Crude Oil	31.04	Aluminium	2.50	Gold	3.68	Wheat	5.18	Live Cattle	3.83
Brent Crude Oil	12.27	Copper	2.51	Silver	0.39	Red Wheat	1.09	Feeder Cattle	0.70
RBOB Gas	4.15	Lead	0.39			Corn	4.85	Lean Hogs	1.97
Heating Oil	4.52	Nickel	0.70			Soybeans	3.44		
GasOil	4.92	Zinc	0.55			Cotton	1.17		
Natural Gas	6.59					Sugar	2.09		
						Coffee	0.99		
						Cocoa	0.49		

Source: GoldmanSachs.com

likely last longer and continue further than many expect. Many trapped long or short traders will admit the end of a trend and close their positions.

EXTREME MOVES

Another approach is to look for significant one-week or multi-week extreme position moves among commercial traders. This group often has base hedging programs in place and won't make drastic moves without a compelling reason. A jump in activity in a given week or month suggests that many commercial traders see a slam-dunk opportunity. The bigger the move, the better.

Stephen E. Briese, longtime COT watcher and author of the book *The Commitments of Traders Bible* (Wiley, 2008) introduced his COT index in a May 1990 *Stocks & Commodities* article. He says that, though each contract has its own unique trading characteristics, it generally pays to more closely watch changes in commercial positions. His COT index compares the current report with the range over the previous three years, allowing him to record highs and lows as the environment changes over time. He looks at the net-short or long position numbers. For example, the commercial traders in Figure 12.1 had 490,101 long contracts and 498,591 short, leaving them 8,490 net short for the week.

$$\text{COT Index} = \frac{100 \times (\text{Current Net} - \text{Minimum Net})}{(\text{Maximum Net} - \text{Minimum Net})}$$

If the maximum in the past three years was 12,500 net-long contracts and the minimum was −21,500 net short, then the week's COT Index should show $100 \times [(-8490 - -21,500)/(12,500 - -21,500)] = 88$ percent. A reading near 0 percent (bearish) or 100 percent (bullish) is extreme; a quick move to that area would be an even stronger signal. A move from a neutral 50 percent to near 90 in two weeks, for instance, would be an especially strong signal. These moves are best seen as trade alerts, because commercial traders tend to anticipate the market.

FIGURE 12.2 shows a Briese chart for the 2006–2007 Nasdaq. Note that small speculators were never a significant factor during that period. Circled points mark times of COT Index readings above 90 percent, which generally forecast good buying opportunities. The

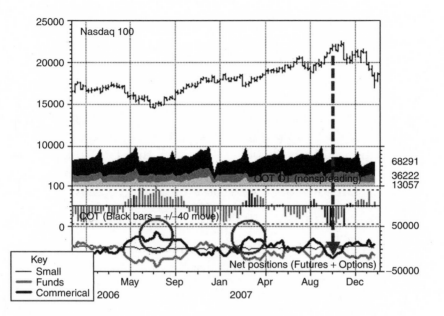

Figure 12.2   Briese COT chart for Nasdaq 100

Source: Bullishreview.com

arrow in early October 2007 warned of a COT reading at 0 percent. Commercial traders hadn't been that net short in a long time.

STAYING OUT OF TROUBLE

Sometimes it doesn't take great detective work to get clues. During the bear market of 2000–2002, investors frequently asked, "Is this the bottom?" Week after week, commercial traders were net short, sometimes by more than 100,000 contracts, or more than $30 billion with an average S&P 500 level of 1250. Only in March 2003 did commercial trader positions turn positive. As a group, they had finally positioned portfolios for a market advance, becoming bullish on stocks and suggesting that other investors would be wise to do likewise.

Riding the Wave—Watching the Large Traders

Some of the world's greatest traders simply follow market trends, especially in commodities where physical supply and demand traits tend to exaggerate moves. Boston Red Sox owner John Henry made his fortune by adding to winning positions and amplifying the few great runs that inevitably come along every year.

Hedge funds dominating the noncommercial/large trader segment are there to make money. Commercial traders may have superior knowledge, but their primary futures goal is to reduce operational volatility, with making money as a secondary consideration

To best ride a trend, traders should track whether large traders are increasing their positions as the current trend persists. A multi-week stall in large trader positions could mean that some investors are exiting trades and booking profits, or that large traders (as a group) are at or approaching their maximum position sizes. A move in the opposite direction could cause a rush for the exits.

Tracking the Shifts—Using COT for Financial Futures

The COT Index offers a numerical (and sometimes visual) way to track position shifts. **FIGURE 12.3** shows net commitments by group for the S&P 500 during 2008. Periods of shifts are circled:

1. **Week of April 1, 2008:** Commercial traders shifted from short 20,000 contracts to long 10,000. The S&P 500 market had sold off from 1350 to 1310 during the last week of March. Commercial traders stayed mildly long for two months as the S&P 500

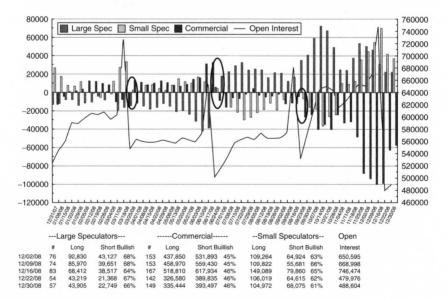

	---Large Speculators---			------Commercial------			--Small Speculators--		Open
	#	Long	Short Bullish	#	Long	Short Buillsh	Long	Short Bullish	Interest
12/02/08	76	92,830	43,127 68%	153	437,850	531,893 45%	109,264	64,924 63%	650,595
12/09/08	74	85,970	39,651 68%	153	458,970	559,430 45%	109,822	55,681 66%	668,998
12/16/08	83	68,412	38,517 64%	167	518,810	617,934 46%	149,089	79,860 65%	746,474
12/22/08	54	43,219	21,368 67%	142	326,580	389,835 46%	106,019	64,615 62%	479,976
12/30/08	57	43,905	22,749 66%	149	335,444	393,497 46%	104,972	68,075 61%	488,604

Figure 12.3   S&P 500 COT report for 2008

Source: cotpricecharts.com

gradually traded up to 1425, and even increased positions in late June.

2. **Week of July 1, 2008:** Commercial traders moved from being long 30,000 contracts (the longest of the year) to short 10,000 contracts. The S&P 500 had tumbled to 1280. Commercial traders stayed modestly short for the next few months as the S&P 500 traded in a range between 1250 and 1300.

3. **Week of September 30, 2008:** Commercial traders moved to the greatest short position of the year, short 30,000 contracts. They kept and increased short positions through the brutal October sell-off, as the S&P 500 traded below 850 late in the month. They nearly doubled their 50,000 short contracts during the week of December 2, 2008 (S&P at 850), suggesting that they felt another market drop was at hand. The year-end timing may also have reflected investment bank hedging, as banks bought enough protection to insure assets through December 31. The market rallied and commercial traders covered most of their short positions during the last week of 2008 and in early 2009 as the S&P 500 moved over 925.

RESOURCES

The Web site for the U.S. Commodity Futures Trading Commission is at www. cftc.gov. CFTC releases the weekly numbers at 3:00 p.m. every Friday, Eastern standard time. Historical information and e-mail subscriptions are freely available at the site.

Edward Chancellor tells the story of the Hunts' silver foray and other accounts of bubbles through history in his book *Devil Take the Hindmost.*

Portfolio manager Michael Masters grabbed headlines when he testified before the Committee on Homeland Security and Governmental Affairs on May 20, 2008, arguing that institutional investors were a significant factor in driving commodity prices higher. His testimony is available at http://hsgac.senate.gov/public/ _files/052008Masters.pdf. Masters was later a key interviewee for a *60 Minutes* piece titled "The Price of Oil," which aired January 11, 2009. Barry Ritholtz's has posted the video and his January 12, 2009, thoughts in the post "What *60 Minutes* Missed on Oil Speculation," available at http://www.ritholtz.com/blog/2009/01/ oil-speculation.

Bloomberg users can find Commitments of Traders data by typing CFTC <Go>. SentimenTrader.com shows all COT charts as part of the broader subscription service. Googling "COT charts" will bring up a few free services, including www. cotpricecharts.com.

Books studying the COT report include *The Commitments of Traders Bible: How to Profit from Insider Market Intelligence* by Steven E. Briese and *Commitments of Traders: Strategies for Tracking the Market and Trading Profitably* by Floyd Upperman.

Chapter 13

Giving Credit to the Bond Market

If you owe the bank $100, that's your problem. If you owe the bank $100 million, that's the bank's problem.

—JEAN PAUL GETTY

The importance of money flows from it being a link between the present and the future.

—JOHN MAYNARD KEYNES

MANY EQUITY INVESTORS consider the bond market a place to preserve capital, not grow it. But the bond market—and the credit market in general—offer indicators that make them well worth following.

To appreciate the indicators the credit markets offer, it's important to understand the differences between equity and debt investors. Equity holders care about return *on* principal. People and organizations that lend money, on the other hand, care about return *of* principal. Because credit providers can receive no more than the face value of a bond or loan, they focus much more on what can go wrong. Equity investors, by contrast, participate in a company's growth, and they spend a lot of time thinking about what can go right. Bondholders' natural skepticism can be a nice counterweight to equity's natural bullishness.

The relationships between bonds with different levels of principal protection give an ongoing barometer of risk tolerance in the credit market. Shifts in lenders' risk tolerance often lead changes in risk tolerance among equity investors.

Bonds can also presage price changes in the equity markets. Credit is an economy's lifeblood. Companies facing tougher lending terms will make less profit in the future, due to higher interest costs, and may have to decline new projects or business because of a lack of cheap capital.

This chapter will look at bond market relationships that offer broader equity market perspectives, review debt indicators specific to analyzing individual securities, and delve into the murky world of credit-default swaps (CDSs) and how it enhances equity forecasts.

Libor and the TED Spread

A bank's balance sheet sets the loans it has extended (assets) against deposits (liabilities) and retained capital. Each bank must keep a reserve (mostly short-term Treasury bills) as a financial cushion against the possibility of loan defaults. Loans and deposits vary over time, so banks sometimes partially fund reserves by borrowing from another bank with excess capital.

The most credit-worthy international banks charge one another the London interbank offered rate (Libor) as an interest rate on large loans. These rates are quoted in monthly increments out to one year; the three-month Eurodollar contract reflects the three-month Libor rate. Libor rates are a commonly used, global lending benchmark for hundreds of billions of mortgages, business loans, hedge fund borrowing, and other interest-rate-sensitive instruments. In normal times, this interbank borrowing rate gives lending banks practically the same result as if they held supersafe U.S. Treasury bonds.

The Treasury-Eurodollar (TED) spread compares the ninety-day interbank lending rate to the three-month Treasury yield; it reveals the perceived credit risk of lending to the largest commercial banks. If the TED spread increases, that signals mistrust between bankers. Banks with excess capital either demand a higher rate or accept a lower return on a supersafe short-term investment, such as a three-month Treasury bond. When bankers are nervous, investors get nervous, too.

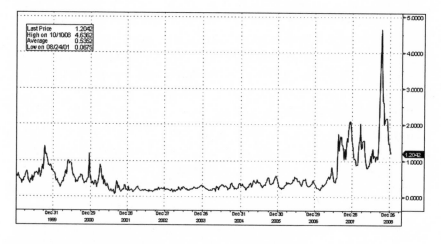

Figure 13.1   Treasury/Libor spread for 1999–2008

Source: Bloomberg

FIGURE 13.1 shows the TED spread for 1999 through 2008.

1. From 1999 through 2001, periodic spikes in the spread signaled temporary times of stress, as the economy wrestled with the recession that followed the dot-com bubble. As with many indicators, sharp, extreme spikes in a fear gauge normally signal a good time to buy, for investors with at least an intermediate time frame.

2. Between 2002 and 2006, there was a long period with no TED spikes, and the spread was under 0.5 percent for extended periods of time. In retrospect, this helps explain the undue lending risks banks took during this time. Perhaps the long quiet stretch drew them into a false sense of security.

3. The initial subprime tremors in mid-2007 set the stage for the market meltdown in 2008. Thought it's not a perfect timing tool, the extreme spikes in this time frame showed high levels of fear.

Corporate Bonds

While the TED spread measures tremors in the banking system and the cost of short-term borrowing, the bond market measures lenders' longer-term risk tolerance. By fund mandate, many bond managers can hold only bonds rated "investment grade" by Standard & Poor's or Moody's. Moody's Baa is the lowest rating that still qualifies as investment grade. Firms with these ratings are good companies but don't have enough financial flexibility to be immune to a slow-down. Many companies pay Baa rates on their bond borrowing and, as discussed in Chapter 7, the rate is an approximation of the risk premium in the stock market.

FIGURE 13.2 shows the spread between Aaa (highest rated) and Baa corporate bonds versus Treasury notes from 1977 to 2008. Periods of low spreads indicate an easier lending environment and (usually) good market performance. (Note the low spreads from 1994 to 1996 and 2005 to 2007.) Rising spreads, however, nudged the stock market down, as the bond market's decreased risk tolerance found its way to equities.

When bond yields fell, they pointed the way toward loosening credit. Better credit availability can be slow to register in the real economy, as once unavailable or prohibitively expensive loans start to become available, and approved projects gradually create jobs. The bond market is typically the first to signal the beginning and end of credit trends.

Junk But Not Trash

Curious investors should also consider the interest rate earned by high-yield bonds, sometimes known as junk bonds. Issuing companies

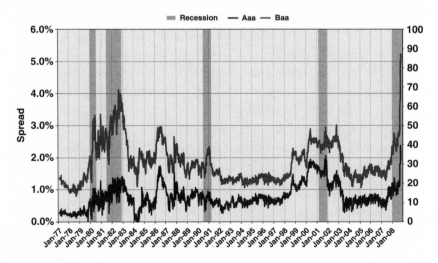

Figure 13.2   Yields of Aaa and Baa corporate bonds versus 30-year Treasury bonds

Source: St. Louis Federal Reserve Bank

are rated as noninvestment or speculative grade, as they have outsized debt, suspect business prospects, or both. Many do not have the financial wherewithal to withstand a recession while continuing to pay bondholders.

In good times, investors often lend freely to these less financially sound companies, sometimes extending credit to lesser borrowers for only a slightly better yield. (Wall Streeters often say that there's nothing more expensive than reaching for yield.) Increasing high-yield spreads suggest that financially strapped companies will have a tougher time paying bondholders, and the rate of bankruptcies—and resulting defaults—will be higher. On the other hand, a declining high-yield spread suggests that once-scarce credit is returning and the stock market is exiting a bear market. Low spreads signal higher risk tolerances and suggest a strong underpinning for all markets—including the stock market. **FIGURE 13.3** shows the amount high-yield issues have yielded over comparable Treasuries from 1997 to 2008.

Lending Officers

Bank lending runs in cycles and often follows trends. When the economy is strong and default rates are low, banks report healthy profits. A few banks offer lower rates or relax their underwriting standards, netting them more business. Eventually, even conservative banks follow suit.

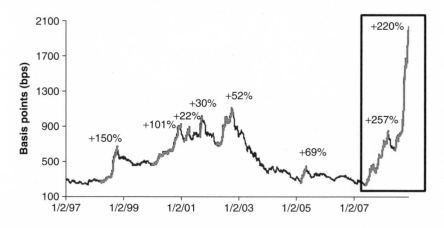

Figure 13.3   High-yield credit spread from 1997 to 2008

Source: Bespoke Investment Group

FIGURE 13.4 shows the January 2009 Federal Reserve report (found at www.federalreserve.gov). Check it to see how easily bankers are extending loans. Areas above the zero line signal an increasing willingness to extend credit; below this line, the data signals a contraction. (As with many other indicators, direction and extremes are the most useful readings one can get from this chart.)

A period of easier credit usually leads to more consumer and business spending and generally a healthy stock market. Credit tightening can have the opposite effect.

Investors can also gauge the availability of individual credit by looking at the market for jumbo mortgage loans. These are loans over the conventional lending limit, which stood at $417,000 for most regions at the end of 2008. Home buyers pay a premium for jumbo loans, because banks can't readily resell the debt. The size of that premium is another measure of credit availability. **FIGURE 13.5** shows the rate jumbo-loan borrowers pay in excess of conventional loan rates.

The two data sets diverged in 2007, when the subprime debt market began to go bad, and the greater market's appetite for debt backed with mortgage loans withered.

Flight to Safety

Some think of gold as an asset that does well during a flight to safety. Gold usually does do well in these periods, but the total gold market isn't big enough to handle every investor in search of a lifeboat. The

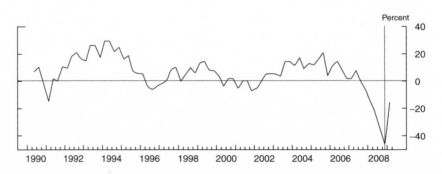

Figure 13.4   Lending officer survey on willingness to extend consumer loans

Source: Federal Reserve Board

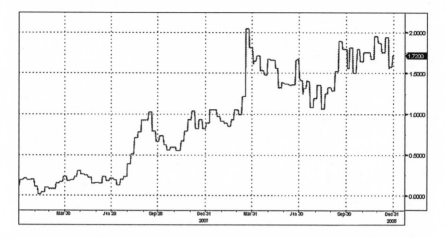

Figure 13.5   Jumbo rates in comparison to conforming rates

Source: Bloomberg

biggest, safest, most liquid instrument for panicky people is U.S. Treasury bonds, often known as T-bills.

On a shorter-term basis, lower spikes in the thirty-day T-bill yield mark days of capitulation and liquidation. On those days, investors are selling off other assets and parking money in ultrasafe T-bills until the smoke clears. They care about preservation, not yield.

FIGURE 13.6 shows the thirty-day T-bill yield and the S&P 500 level during 2008, a year filled with alarming financial events. Because the Federal Reserve cut rates to zero in the fall, there was literally no room left for the thirty-day rate to spike downwards. In this case, other Treasury yields, such as that of the 10-year bond, may serve as a better spike indicator.

From Spreads to Slopes—The Yield Curve

To this point, the discussion has focused on the difference between government and corporate bond rates, typically in 10-year instruments. It's also wise to review rates at different maturities: thirty days, three months, three years, thirty years.

The yield curve is a visual representation of the interest rates on government securities at varying maturities. **FIGURE 13.7** shows the yield curve for October 2, 2006, and October 1, 2007 and 2008.

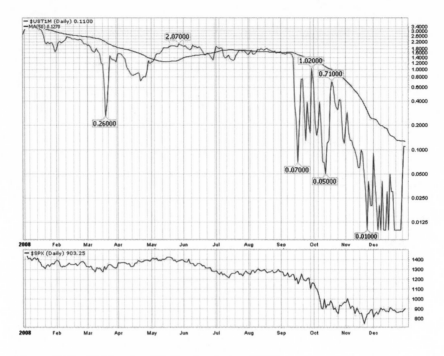

Figure 13.6   Thirty-day T-bill rate during 2008

Source: Chart courtesy of StockCharts.com (http://stockcharts.com)

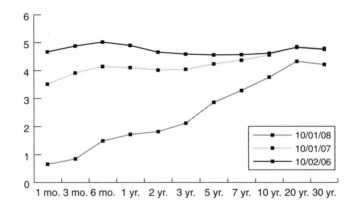

Figure 13.7   Treasury yield curve on October 1, 2006, 2007, and 2008

Source: www.ustreas.gov

Notice the different shapes over just three years. The yield curve in
2006 was flat to slightly inverted: rates were basically the same at all
maturities. There were times in 2006 when the government paid

less to borrow for ten years than for three months; at those points, the yield curve was inverted.

Banks make money by lending long and borrowing short, taking in deposits—which they must pay back on demand—and lending on long-term assets, such as home mortgages. Bank profits come from the spread between short- and long-term rates. With little difference between the two, there's less profit on each loan. Over time, a flat or inverted yield curve usually slows the economy—a desirable goal when the Fed is concerned about long-term inflation. In 2006, the Fed raised short-term rates in an effort to slow or stop the housing market. Eventually, of course, it succeeded.

The 2007 curve was normal: gently curved, with short-term rates slightly lower than longer rates. The Fed had cut rates on signs of economic weakness and dwindling concern over inflation. The stock market was hitting new highs. Fed cuts had helped relieve the pressure of an inverted yield curve, but bank lending still wasn't overly profitable, and many equity investors were cautious.

The yield curve on December 15, 2008, when the Fed took the historic step of cutting the Fed funds rate to basically 0 percent in an attempt to boost the economy, was fairly steep again. Ten-year bonds yielded a historically low 2.4 percent. Banks used "free" Fed money to buy 10-year government bonds, because consumer and corporate loan default rates made them too nervous to lend. Many equity investors were cautious.

To see the current yield curve slope, use the Market Center tab on Bloomberg.com. For a time-lapse movie of the yield curve through time, go to http://fixedincome.fidelity.com/fi/FIHistoricalYield. Daily yield curve changes are nearly imperceptible. Given enough time, however, yield curve changes leave their mark on the economy and stock market.

A Different Look

FIGURE 13.8 shows a different view of the yield curve, one that considers only four Treasury bond yields during the ten years between 1999 and 2009. This view helps demonstrate how aggressive the Federal Reserve has been, and shows the gradual reactions of other maturities along the yield curve.

One can see that the flat yield curve in this figure occurs when all four rates (3-month, 5-year, 10-year and 30-year) are all close together. At this time, the Fed was tightening credit and trying to slow the economy, because it was concerned about an overly strong economy and the possibility of rising inflation. Many market participants argued that the inverted yield curve would not slow the economy, as it had in the past.

As the Fed aggressively cut rates, the yield spread widened. Investors preferred the 30-year bond in a slowing economy, amid diminished inflationary prospects. In mid 2003, the bond markets recognized an economic recovery, and all three publicly determined yields (5-, 10-, and 30-year) jumped. They lost value as the prospect of a strong economy suggested that value-destroying inflation was on the way, and that stocks represented a good investment alternative.

The flat yield curve returned and stayed for more than a year between early 2006 and mid 2007. In 2008, the Fed ended at 0 percent, trying once again to jumpstart the economy with low rates.

Liquidity and VIX

In a publicly available research brief posted on March 22, 2006, BCA Research noted that, when the Fed raises rates, the VIX typically rises as well. Researchers found that increases in the Fed funds rate reduce liquidity and boost the market's uncertainty about future earnings growth.

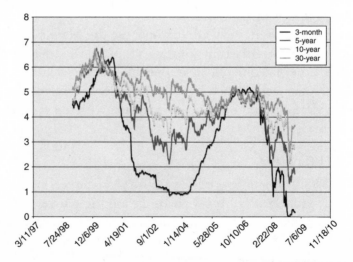

Figure 13.8   3-month, 5-year, 10-year and 30-year yields through time

Data Source: www.federalreserve.com

Professor Shiu-Sheng Chen, of National Taiwan University, looked at the predictive power of the yield curve in his March 2008 paper "Predicting the Bear Stock Market: Macroeconomic Variables as Leading Indicators." He considered monthly data from 1957 to 2007, asking whether the inflation rate, money supply, economic aggregate output, and unemployment rate could individually forecast the onset of an equity bear market. He found that

- Bull markets tend to last twenty months. Bear markets typically last 6.7 months.
- Yield curve spread and inflation rate are the best predictors of a bear market but do not predict its severity.
- A simple switching strategy between stocks and bonds, based on the modeled probability of a coming bear market, substantially beat a buy-and-hold equity strategy over that fifty-year period.

Forecasting Bankruptcy

Bankers and bondholders have first rights to a company's assets. If business gets really bad, these investors will step in to protect whatever value remains. Buildings, inventory, and accounts receivable can all be liquidated to return some value to creditors. It's not a pleasant process, but it helps continue the cycle of innovation and growth that an economy needs to develop.

Individual bond prices can help tell equity traders how worried bondholders are about a company's ability to repay its debt. At distressed yield levels—more than 10 percent above the Treasury rate for the corresponding maturity—the bond market handicaps the odds of bankruptcy, forecasting the number of bond payments investors will receive and the likely liquidation value they'll get in bankruptcy court.

Stockholders rarely receive money from a bankrupt company, so equity traders are wise to consider any warning the bond market might issue. If a company's bonds yield 18 percent and the stock is trading at $10, one security is probably mispriced—in most cases, the stock. Many hedge funds buy the company's bonds and short its stock in this situation.

The z-score is another indicator of future bankruptcy risk. Edward Altman, a Nobel Prize winner, financial economist, and professor at New York University's Stern School of Business, developed a model in 1968 that measures a nonfinancial company's health by looking at five different financial ratios.

$$\text{z-score} = 1.2a + 1.4b + 3.3c + 0.6d + 1.0e,$$

where
a = Working Capital/Total Assets
b = Retained Earnings/Total Assets
c = Earnings before Interest and Tax (EBIT)/Total Assets
d = Equity Market Capitalization/Total Assets
e = Annual Sales/Total Assets

Higher numbers represent stronger financial health. A score of 3.0 or above signals a small likelihood of bankruptcy in the next two years. A score lower than 1.8 indicates financial distress and a greater likelihood that the company is heading for bankruptcy. Scores between 1.8 and 3.0 are inconclusive.

A quick review shows the importance of these key financial ratios to general corporate health.

- **Working Capital to Total Assets:** Working capital is the excess of current assets (primarily cash, accounts receivable, and inventory) over current liabilities (mostly accounts payable and short-term debt). It's a measure of a firm's ability to pay its bills.
- **Retained Earnings to Total Assets:** Companies with a high ratio often have a record of financing themselves through operating profits, rather than through borrowing. In many cases, they can withstand a rough economic patch.
- **EBIT to Total Assets:** This ratio measures a company's ability to earn a high return on assets, the hallmark of an effective, successful enterprise.
- **Market Capitalization to Total Liabilities:** A company with an equity value much larger than its debts suggests financial strength and flexibility.
- **Sales to Total Assets:** Another ratio that measures how effectively management uses assets to generate return.

The z-score is of less use for newer companies with little or low earnings, which will have low scores, or for firms with large write-offs.

Fraud also skews z-scores, but still gives a better idea of overall company strength than does earnings per share.

An example of this is in **TABLE 13.1**. It tracks WorldCom in the three years leading up to its July 2002 bankruptcy filing, which was forced in part by fraud. These numbers are from SEC 10-K filings.

WorldCom's most serious accounting fraud incorporated taking regular operating expenses (such as ongoing maintenance) and treating them as a capital expenditure to be amortized over time. The fraud pumped up near-term earnings and overstated assets, showing an unrealistic operating margin and profit level while lowering return on assets. Overstating profits lifted one measure but lowered three others. A deteriorating z-score should nudge investors to analyze a company more deeply.

Bloomberg users can use the AZS function to see a company's score. Find a z-score calculator at www.creditguru.com/CalcAltZ.shtml.

Credit-Default Swaps—Bond Insurance

Bondholders face two risks. First, an issuer may go bankrupt and default on the bond, a possibility known as default risk. Second,

Table 13.1   Z-scores of WorldCom, 1999–2001

Financial Ratio	1999	2000	2001
Working capital/total assets	−0.09	−0.08	0.00
Retained earnings/ total assets	−0.02	0.03	0.04
EBIT/total assets	0.09	0.08	0.02
Market cap/total liabilities	3.7	1.2	0.50
Sales/total assets	0.51	0.42	0.30
Z-score	*2.50*	*1.40*	*0.85*
Revenues (millions)	35,908	39,090	35,179
Operating income (millions)	7,888	8,153	3,514
Earnings per share	$1.40	$1.43	$0.48
December 31 stock price	$51.36	$13.50	$14.38

Source: Securities and Exchange Commission

interest rates may rise, making a bond less attractive and depressing its price. This is known as interest-rate risk.

Credit-default swaps (CDSs) insure against default risk. Typically purchased from an investment bank's CDS desk, CDS contracts vary in length. In case of default, bondholders settle a contract through either physical settlement, in which they deliver the bonds and receive full face value, or a cash settlement, in which the investment bank sends bondholders the difference between a bond's current value and its full face value.

Bondholders buy CDS contracts, of course, but one doesn't have to own a company's bond in order to purchase a CDS. Hedge funds sometimes buy CDSs outright, betting that a bond will lose value. That same hedge fund can sell a CDS contract—effectively writing an insurance contract—if it feels the market is overly pessimistic about the prospects of a bond defaulting. In this case, as with futures contracts, the hedge fund must post collateral with the broker facilitating the trade.

There is no liquid secondary market for CDSs. As an example, an investor might pay an annual 2 percent for $10 million in protection, plus up-front fees in some cases. That rate can change with the bond's perceived risk. If the original investor thinks the cost has gotten too high, he or she can effectively sell the insurance policy by selling an offsetting CDS contract.

The CDS market was valued around $1 trillion in 1998, and exploded to $62 trillion in 2008. Contracts generally expire or are paid out, so the true exposure is substantially less. But in this unregulated market, no one really knows. Bear Stearns received a 2008 government bailout in part because of its tremendous exposure to the CDS market. Regulators worried that the company's failure could bring the entire financial system to its knees.

In retrospect, the equity market was slow to recognize the imminent collapse of Bear Stearns and other financial giants, including Fannie Mae, AIG, and Merrill Lynch. CDS prices, however, did foresee the high risk that these companies would fail, as reflected in the skyrocketing cost of CDS contracts on the firms' bonds. The cost of insuring $10 million in debt issued by an average financial sector company went from $20,000 in June 2006 to $303,000 in June 2008. The cost for insuring debt issued by companies in the auto and housing industries went from $149,000 to $525,000 during the same time period—reflecting an increase in risk levels, but not on the same scale as the increase experienced by financial companies.

This kind of financial performance suggested that credit-default swaps are a potential predictor of company performance. In an October 7, 2008 report titled "Credit Default Swaps: Do Widening Spreads Lead the Stocks?," Alliance Bernstein senior analyst Adam Parker examined this question. Parker and his team concluded that

- Changes in the price of a five-year CDS contract were more important than absolute CDS pricing in predicting future stock declines.
- This signal offers a lead time of about sixty days, making this either a shorter-term trading indicator, or a warning that long-term investors should sell what they own or stay away from the stock.
- The stocks that had the greatest ninety-day change in CDS price (especially the top 10 percent) had the worst relative return over the next sixty days.

The Bernstein report concluded that a sharp jump in CDS price typically leads declining equity performance by about two months. Time will tell whether this indicator persists, now that more people

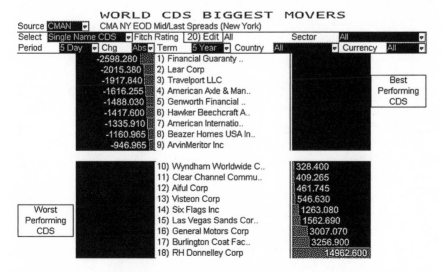

Figure 13.9   CDS Biggest Movers as of January 13, 2009

Source: Bloomberg

are paying attention. Changes in the CDS market, such as more pricing transparency, may also alter its value as an indicator.

FIGURE 13.9 shows a Bloomberg screen reporting largest five-day changes in CDS prices. Those on top represent firms with declining CDS prices and therefore short-term improving credit profiles. The firms on the bottom are companies with the greatest increase in CDS prices and therefore short-term deteriorating credit outlooks, according to CDS traders.

RESOURCES

Regulators and traders have discussed standardizing CDS contracts and moving the market to an exchange, to add transparency. Until that happens, investors need access to a bank's CDS desk or a Bloomberg terminal (function CDSD) to get a CDS quote. Traders may also see CDS levels mentioned in a financial news story as an indicator of a company's perceived strength or weakness.

Bloomberg.com provides a current reading and historical chart for the TED spread at http://www.bloomberg.com/apps/cbuilder?ticker1=.TEDSP%3AIND or Google "Bloomberg Ted Spread".

The Federal Reserve Bank of St. Louis offers a wealth of economic data, including historical interest rates at its Web site, Federal Reserve Economic Data (FRED), at http://research.stlouisfed.org/fred2.

Among other sources of lending rates, www.bankrate.com lists a variety of loan products with current and historical yields for each. For historical graphs, go to www.bankrate.com/funnel/graph. A graph of the spread between jumbo and conforming 30-year fixed-rate mortgages for the past year is available at www.banx.com.

A variety of free online z-score calculators can be found by Googling "Altman z-score calculator".

Michael Shedlock (Mish) writes a popular blog called Mish's Global Economic Trend Analysis (http://globaleconomicanalysis.blogspot.com) and will occasionally comment on the current credit markets, among other qualitative factors he feels are important. Prieur du Plessis is another blogger (Investment Postcards from Cape Town at www.investmentpostcards.com) who frequently reviews signals from the credit markets.

Blogs specifically focused on the credit market include Calculated Risk (www.calculatedriskblog.com) and Accrued Interest (accruedint.blogspot.com). The managers (including Bill Gross and Mohamed El-Erian) of the world's largest bond manager, PIMCO, regularly post their commentary and views at www.pimco.com.

Chapter 14

Money In, Money Out (IPOs, Secondaries, Mergers, Buybacks, and Dividends)

If the lady wants green shoes, sell her green shoes.

—old Wall Street saying

MOST OF THIS BOOK considers the ebb and flow of investors' appetite for risk, a measurement of *demand* for stocks. This chapter will explore the dynamic of companies coming to the capital markets, as an indicator of stock *supply*.

A rising stock supply is a market headwind, often stretching available investor funds to buy additional shares coming from initial public offerings (IPOs) and secondary offerings. This chapter discusses IPO implications, stock buybacks (which reduce the number of shares available, thereby supporting stock prices), and other factors to consider when thinking of the market's supply-and-demand dynamics.

Increasing Supply—The IPO Process

For most investors, an IPO is a beginning, the first day they can freely trade a firm's shares. For the company, however, the IPO marks the end of a fairly long journey. The process of going public takes time. A company must reach a certain size and have both a sufficient operating history and a compelling growth outlook. It must be willing and able to assume the significantly higher costs and stricter regulator requirements incurred by publicly traded companies. Along the way, managers must consider and then dismiss the option of selling their company to a larger competitor or private equity firm, instead of pursuing an IPO.

A firm must then hear from several investment banks, all eager to manage the IPO process. The company will consider each bank's standing with institutional investors and ability to place new shares at the best possible price. The successful bank must also be able to support management in telling its story—an area where it may conflict with analysts, who have the tough job of simultaneously supporting investment bankers in getting the business, currying favor with company management, and maintaining the objectivity that institutional investors trust.

The winning bank will charge the company between 5 percent and 7 percent of the money raised. In return, the bank will help determine a good time for the IPO. Because an IPO can take a month or two from beginning to end, it will do best in a fairly stable, nonvolatile market that allows the bank to set and stick to a proposed offering price.

The bank also conducts due diligence research on the company and their competitive position, finds similar companies, and determines an appropriate valuation range. This research forms the background of the IPO prospectus, the legal document laying out all available information an investor should consider before buying shares. The investment bank is liable if it is not thorough or intentionally leaves out key items.

The investment bank then takes management on a "road show," presenting the company to key potential investors in several cities. Both bank and company benefit from a smaller, more committed group of investors. Committed investors are more likely to hold the newly issued shares for a long time, which creates the stable owner base that firms prefer. As a result, large institutional clients, which can get a performance bump from post-IPO price increases, are the main buyers in most IPOs.

Investors consider the research, take management's measure, and weigh whether the proposed offering price is fair. If they feel it's a good bargain, they will tell their bank representatives how many shares they would like to own. IPO investors take a risk in buying a company with a limited sense of how it will trade on the open market. Investment banks must strike a balance between getting a good price for the company (their client) and providing a good profit opportunity for the investor (who is also their client). Investors likely already have trading business with the bank, and will remember a poorly managed IPO.

At the road show's conclusion, the investment bank looks at the orders in hand. If there is *huge* demand, the bank may raise the offering price and/or increase the percent of the company to be sold to the public. To manage stock supply, the investment bank contractually prevents insiders from selling additional stock for a certain period of time, usually one hundred and eighty days.

Understanding that process helps investors find signals in IPOs in general, as well as in specific IPOs.

EXAMINING IPOS FOR CLUES

Lawyers write a company's preliminary prospectus (called a "red herring," for the section—printed in red—that states that the company is not trying to sell shares before the prospectus gets SEC approval), which can be painfully boring to read. Pay attention to the crucial financial statements and to the section dedicated to "warning factors," which includes a laundry list of what can go wrong. Much of this is boilerplate language found in every prospectus, including obvious statements such as "our company's operations could be significantly impacted by a nuclear war." But the notes may also contain information about significant, company-specific issues. Maybe there's a patent dispute that could be the company's ruin if a court decision doesn't go their way. Perhaps the firm has one or two customers that make up more than 50 percent of their sales—heaven help them if they lose those customers, or if those clients use their outsized influence to negotiate better prices. A section on warning factors appears in each public company's annual SEC filing (known as a 10-K), and it's often revealing to see what has changed from the previous year. Such footnotes clued short sellers into the off-balance sheet financing arms that eventually brought down Enron.

Also read the lock-up provisions and the list of stock amounts and ownership. A short lock-up period (say, ninety days) suggests that insiders are anxious to sell. And an insider list dominated by venture capitalists, who provide financing to early-stage companies and use the IPO process as a way of returning cash to *their* investors, may suggest a steady source of stock sales after the lockup time has passed. Venture capitalists make a living by picking winners among start-ups, not by managing portfolios of publicly held securities.

An understanding of supply and demand has helped some investors get rich. In the midst of the Internet bubble, some stocks rocketed to unsustainable valuations. Stocks that should have traded at $12 per share were up $12 per share in a *day*. Short sellers went out of business trying to pick the top. Scores of traders made millions by following the trend; many gave it back when the bubble collapsed.

Investor Sir John Templeton, then in his eighties, could see that these valuations were not sustainable. He combined fundamental analysis with a study of IPO lockup provisions. Templeton recognized that an irrational demand for a limited stock supply was one reason stocks raced even higher for companies with cutting-edge technology or other market niches. He researched stocks, shorting the flawed ones as these stocks drew near their lockup expiration. He knew that the irrational demand could continue, but would finally be met with more supply when insiders and founding venture capitalists sold shares to the public. (Other traders used this strategy, too.) While other dedicated short sellers lost their shirt, Templeton made millions by understanding that the demand and supply of a stock are sometimes more important than fundamental valuation.

As Templeton found, measuring IPO quantity and quality can give clues to investor stock demand. Web sites such as ipohome. com and biz.yahoo.com/ipo/ track this market.

FIGURE 14.1 shows IPO issuance by month. Note bulges where investment banks raced to supply the market with newly public companies. A long-term market top was building, but the good times lasted for quite a while.

QUALITY VERSUS QUANTITY

Also note which companies go public and in which sectors. A few private equity firms and hedge funds, including The Blackstone Group (BX), Fortress Investment Group (FIG), and Man Group (MAN on the London Exchange), took the unusual step of going public themselves. Their IPOs served mainly to offer firm principals an opportunity to cash out part of their ownership stake, which they did.

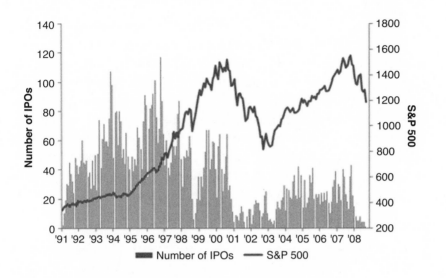

Figure 14.1 Initial public offerings by month, 1991–2009

Source: Bespoke Investment Group

When these stocks quickly sank below their IPO prices, it was one sign that investor demand for these financial firms had been met.

The summer of 2007 saw IPOs for several ethanol companies, as government mandates and price supports ensured ready buyers for ethanol. Stocks such as Pacific Ethanol (partially owned by Bill Gates) and Aventine Renewable Energy earned huge profits on the spread between the low price of corn and the high price of gasoline. Making ethanol is fairly easy, and soon ethanol plants were sprouting up throughout the Corn Belt. Sure enough, supply caught up with demand for both ethanol and ethanol stocks. Corn prices shot up, eliminating the profit margin. Ethanol stocks plummeted.

The year 2008 was a crazy year for commodities; staples such as oil, wheat, and nickel doubled and tripled in price. Eric Sprott, a respected commodity portfolio manager, reported terrific 2007 hedge fund and mutual fund returns through Sprott Incorporated's (SII, Toronto exchange) investments in energy, metals, and mining companies. His firm earned $42 million in advisory fees that year. On May 15, 2008, investors snapped up a CDN $200 million IPO ($10 per share) for 13 percent of his company, valuing his firm at $1.5 billion.

Most money-management firms sport price/earnings ratios of 10 to 15; a year or two of poor portfolio returns can cause clients to pull their assets. Sprott Incorporated sported a nearly 40 price/earnings ratio, an astronomical number for a money-management firm that owned no significant hard assets. Sprott's high IPO valuation could only pay off if Sprott continued growing assets under management at a high rate, which could only happen if money continued to flow into specialty commodity funds. That, however, was not in the long-term cards. It would be a few more months before the broad commodity asset class reached a top and began its decline.

Secondary Offerings

Once a company is public it can register and sell more stock. A firm's investment bank typically checks with large investors to gauge their interest in buying a big block at a discount to the current market price. If a stock declines on big volume with no apparent news, this may indicate that big investors know that a secondary offering is in the works.

WHEN THEY HAVE TO

CEOs typically offer stock at two times: when they have to offer it (they need the money), and when they would be stupid not to offer it (the stock is overpriced).

A healthy company consistently finances expansion plans with cash flow. An industry with seasonal swings, such as the retail sector, can get bank or vendor financing ahead of a predictable surge in their business activity. Firms can also raise money by selling noncore assets.

It makes sense to issue stock to finance a large, well-considered merger, or a large, transformational project that will propel the company forward. In these cases, CEOs work to persuade shareholders that management's plan is a wise one.

In most other circumstances, investors faced with a secondary stock offering will question why their ownership should be diluted. A secondary stock offering suggests that bank financing is hard to come by, or that no one will pay a decent price for company assets.

Money center banks in 2008 are a case in point. These banks reported huge losses as shaky loans defaulted. Many tried to sell their loan portfolios, but found no workable market for the mortgages they had written to financially stretched borrowers. The remaining option was to sell a piece of the bank on favorable terms to foreign investors. Large banks such as Citigroup (C) and Morgan Stanley (MS) went to sovereign wealth funds in Abu Dhabi and Qatar, offering big blocks of discounted ownership. The strategy did raise needed equity, but write-offs swamped the extra liquidity.

On April 21, 2008, another example occurred. National City announced a $7 billion secondary offering. That surprised investors, who had expected a premium buyout offer from another bank. The stock promptly fell 25 percent on the announcement. Potential buyers, such as Warburg Pincus, KeyCorp, and Fifth Third Bank, had apparently decided that National City's price was too high, despite the stock's 75 percent decline over the previous year. By issuing more stock, National City signaled that it also thought the stock was too high—or that it simply had no other way to raise cash. This dynamic played out across the banking sector in the spring of 2008. Only when Wells Fargo trumped Citigroup's bid for Wachovia in October 2008 did buyers find enduring value in a large, distressed bank. Financial stocks, however, continued to decline.

WHEN THEY'RE STUPID NOT TO

Be wary when a stock is riding high and a company issues secondary stock to raise cash for "general corporate purposes." Perhaps the money will fund a pending acquisition. If not, however, a secondary may take place because the market is hungry for more shares, and the CEO wants the proceeds for future deployment. If the company does spend it, it may make risky acquisitions or reach for the most speculative internal projects, in order to satisfy investors' higher growth expectations. Either way, it's probably not a good time for a long-term investor to bid up the stock.

FIGURE 14.2A AND FIGURE 14.2B show the price charts for Genko Shipping (GNK) and TBS International (TBSI) during 2008. Both companies are bulk dry shippers. Comprising the backbone of global commerce, these companies lease ships to haul dry commodities such as wheat or iron ore. As global trade exploded and China showed an unquenchable demand for commodities, shipment prices increased dramatically. GNK's net income went from $54 million in 2005 to $107 million in 2007.

The charts in Figure 14.2a and Figure 14.2b show the points at which the two firms conducted secondary offerings during 2008.

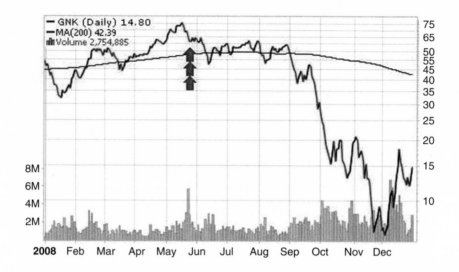

Figure 14.2a   2008 price charts for Genko Shipping with secondary offerings noted

Source: Chart courtesy of StockCharts.com (http://stockcharts.com)

Figure 14.2b   2008 price charts for TBS International with secondary offerings noted

Source: Chart courtesy of StockCharts.com (http://stockcharts.com)

Company executives had seen the shipping cycle play out, and likely wanted to bolster the balance sheet with even more cash for the inevitable demand reduction, or the introduction of new, competing ships. Insiders from both companies sold sizable amounts of stock in the offering. The stock sold off in the week between the offering's announcement and the actual stock sale, suggesting that the company needed a greater discount to attract sufficient demand.

A secondary's price indicates a price level attracting a healthy buying interest. When a stock breaks through this level (or the IPO price), even months later, it suggests that investor interest has waned. The stock may decline further before generating more buying interest. Many times this happens when growth stock investors, who are generally less price sensitive, sour on a company's outlook and sell the stock. The next natural block of investors is value investors, who are very price conscious and focus less on a company's growth prospects. If a company has been a growth stock darling for some time and enjoyed a terrific price run, its stock may fall considerably before reaching a price point that attracts value-oriented investors.

But not every secondary offering indicates a stock price top. Consider Google (GOOG), which issued more than 14 million shares for $4.2 billion in September 2005 at $295 per share for "general corporate purposes." (The company already had $3 billion in cash and was generating tremendous cash flow from ongoing operations.) Rumors swirled that the firm would use the money to buy up smaller Web companies.

But this secondary issue did a poor job of calling a top. The stock powered to over $700 per share in late 2007 before falling below $300 in October 2008. For traders and momentum investors, a stock's reaction to a secondary can signal latent demand. In this case, the discount was only 2.6 percent to the $303 stock price at the secondary completion, and the stock climbed by more than 6 percent in the week following the announced offering. Investors were hungry for stock, and the secondary offering suggested a strong floor for Google at this price point.

Mergers and Buyouts

Just like IPOs, mergers often happen in fits and starts. In an industry ripe for consolidation, companies may hold back, hoping to buy rather than be bought. Once one CEO makes a move, many other firms follow suit. A whole sector may rise after a significant new merger is announced, because costs go down and competitive pressures from underbidding firms may ease.

A healthy overall deal market also suggests good times ahead. Like insiders buying their own stock, mergers suggest that people in the know see value in acquiring other companies. In the 1980s, T. Boone Pickens and other "corporate raiders" figured that oil was cheaper on Wall Street than in Texas. In 1983, Pickens, then CEO of the small energy firm Mesa Petroleum, started buying stock in Gulf Oil when the value of Gulf was about $6 billion; Mesa eventually made an offer to take over the much larger company. A range of counteroffers ensued before Chevron closed the bidding with an offer valued at $13.2 billion. These expert oilmen knew that energy companies were severely undervalued.

In 2006 and 2007, private equity firms executed massive, leveraged deals. Public company cash flows were healthy enough to support acquirer debt, particularly given the prevailing low interest rates. Private equity returns attracted more institutional money, banks lowered credit standards, and stockholders benefited from high company valuations, even for marginal firms.

Anxious to avoid being bought and facing investor pressure, companies took on huge debt loads to accomplish their own acquisitions or pay out large, one-time dividends. Loaded with debt, they were no longer juicy takeover targets.

FIGURE 14.3 shows the quarterly merger and acquisition activity in the United States from March 1999 through March 2009. The trailing four quarter average is also shown. One can see activity peaked at the top of the market in early 2000 before bottoming during 2003 before reaching a new peak during the second quarter of 2007. Money coming into the markets, whether through buybacks or buyouts, helps support and lift prices; money flowing out does the opposite.

Buybacks

Stocks typically jump 3 percent to 6 percent on a buyback announcement. Management has declared that they are a buyer with deep pockets, able to set a temporary price floor. But an announcement is not an ironclad pledge. Management can decide against

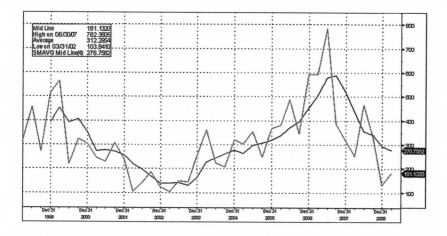

Figure 14.3   U.S. Merger and Acquisition activity

Source: Bloomberg

buying back *any* shares of stock. A buyback announcement could be merely a marketing ploy. Check to see if the company has a history of completing their buyback announcements.

In a buyback, executives are typically held to the same rules that govern insider trading. A lack of follow-through could also reflect a pending corporate development, such as a sale or merger. Or perhaps business is suffering, and the company has decided to conserve its resources.

In a quickly growing company, share buybacks can signal a plateau. The firm has more cash on hand than it can prudently allocate to new, high-return projects. Management in this case deserves credit for not wasting capital, choosing instead to return it to shareholders. Even so, the company will likely see slower growth in the quarters to come.

As with insider activity, buyback size matters. A very large buyback is a louder signal and a greater source of buying demand.

PUTTING LIPSTICK ON A PIG

Earnings per share is an easy measurement of a company's performance, and some investors look no further. Bear in mind, however, that a management team in the midst of a business slowdown can turn lower profits into higher earnings per share by buying back shares at a greater rate than the one at which profits are decreasing.

The self-limiting ploy doesn't really return value to shareholders; it provides value only to those selling shares. To spot it, look at a firm's sales, margins, and operating earnings. Be especially wary if management is itself selling into the effects of this self-induced boost.

Not every buyback reduces shares outstanding. Some merely soak up shares issued through options grants. The share count stays unchanged, despite *a lot* of shareholder cash going out the door. A good analyst adjusts prior income statements to increase the compensation expense for cash spent on buybacks. In some cases, there's not much left over.

Qualcomm (QCOM) offers an example. The cell phone infrastructure company had a good year in 2006, earning $2.47 billion ($1.49 per share). During the year, the firm bought back 34 million shares for $1.5 billion, an average price of $44.11 per share. Qualcomm started with 1.638 billion shares outstanding and ended with 1.659 billion shares, adding 21 million additional shares through options grants and some small acquisitions. In practical terms, then, Qualcomm delivered much less than the reported earnings to shareholders that year.

Technology companies are known for relatively generous employee options packages. Options have become an expected compensation component, a key talent lure and a way to clearly tie employee compensation to shareholder returns. Despite more transparent options accounting rules enacted in the last few years, it's often difficult to determine how much value outside shareholders realize in a buyback conducted by a firm with a substantial options program.

BUYBACKS THAT MAKE SENSE

Boom times bring firms a cash influx that many shareholders will want put to work, rather than letting it sit on the balance sheet. Some investors may clamor for an increased dividend, a one-time payout, or a large stock buyback. Management, on the other hand, may prefer to keep cash available as an operational shock absorber during the inevitable bumps in the road. In tough times, firms can use cash to expand while competitors are retrenching, to acquire assets at bargain prices, to hire great talent, or to buy back stock at attractive levels. Vocal short-term investors can make it difficult for management to keep that perspective.

Exxon Mobil (XOM) earned tens of billions during the oil bull market. Congress criticized the company for its excessive profits, and some investors berated the firm, calling dividends too small and buybacks insufficient. Exxon managers, however, kept a steady, long-term outlook. They continued to operate on the assumption that oil would bring a selling price of about $50 per barrel over the long term, a seemingly too conservative assumption when oil was selling for more than $100 a barrel. When oil dropped under $50, the firm was in an enviable position, able to continue its ongoing exploration program, purchase abandoned assets from overleveraged competitors, and potentially acquire other companies at attractive prices, while still paying investors a dividend. Keeping a long-term focus worked for Exxon.

Dividends—The Other Use of Cash

Dividends can be the unsung hero of investor returns. They are management's third option in deploying profits, alongside stock buyback and business reinvestment. Dividends, which are a tangible reflection of a firm's ongoing operational health, signal management's *long-term* view of sustainable money flow. Firms that regularly increase dividends signal a steadily growing and profitable business. In some cases, management might be wise to suspend a dividend program in order to conserve capital, but companies are loath to do so. The move sends a public signal that the firm's sustainable cash flow dropped—or that management believes it will drop in the very near future.

RESOURCES

Web sites such as www.ipohome.com and http://biz.yahoo.com/ipo/ track the initial public offering market.

The online *Wall Street Journal* (www.wsj.com) contains a wealth of information under the Market Data tab. IPOs and stock offerings can be found under the Calendars & Economy subheading.

Chapter **15**

Tracking the Trailblazers

I start where the last man left off.

—THOMAS EDISON

EVERY TRADE HAS a buyer and a seller. One person is happy to be the new owner of an asset that may appreciate in value, the other is happy to receive the cash. And they can both be right, depending on their individual goals, needs, and investment philosophies.

Anytime you trade, it's good practice to know why *you're* making a particular move and to consider why another smart, perceptive person is doing the exact opposite. Understanding the other side of the trade helps investors develop a healthy regard for opposing views.

This chapter will explain how traders can find out who is buying and selling and can make educated guesses about the reasons behind the trades. We'll discuss the pressures and incentives felt by different investor groups, and explain why their trades may point to opportunities for other market participants.

A Random Walk

In his famous book *A Random Walk Down Wall Street* (Norton, 1973), Burton Malkiel writes that, if one thousand people flip a coin ten times, mathematics suggest that *one* person would land heads each time. Not understanding the math, some would hail this person as an expert coin flipper. Malkiel makes the case for index investing by arguing that *on average*, active money managers cannot beat the market.

He has a point, of course. But a few investors post market-beating returns over time. That necessarily short list includes

- **Warren Buffett:** Investors who follow Buffett have found that he has shown that a practice of buying whatever he buys, even well after his actual purchase date, has delivered twice the S&P 500 return over the last thirty years. He may not *always* be right, but his positions are always well considered.
- **John Paulson:** Paulson runs the multibillion-dollar Paulson Funds and is best known for his early call on the extent of the financial crisis. His fund made billions betting that mortgage securities would fail in 2007 and that banks would suffer as a result in 2008. Paulson is an example of someone who has recently been very right *and* supports that case with hard evidence.
- **Wilbur Ross:** Ross has been a distressed-debt investor for decades. He has bought companies out of bankruptcy court and made a substantial living by doing so. Ross's researchers do *thousands* of hours of work to find business sectors that trade at throwaway prices, yet have enduring value.

All three investors have a demonstrated flexibility to go where value is, as well as a focus on strong, lasting trends. It's possible to piggyback on their hard work and co-opt their ideas as one's own.

CHECKING IN WITH THE SEC
Institutional investors who manage more than $100 million must file a form 13F within forty-five days of the end of each quarter. This information can be stale. A fund could buy stock on January 3 and report it as part of the March 31 holdings on May 14. Many funds change their *entire* portfolio during the course of a year, sometimes more than once, so it can be dangerous to assume that a fund still owns a stock by the time it files a report. But these filings can help investors find long-term stockholders with reputations for doing terrific research before entering positions.

WEAK VERSUS STRONG
Watch quarterly holding changes among a stock's top owners. Some mutual funds are growth investors, adding to positions as long as a company shows strong results, but selling quickly when a company's

growth trajectory tails off. When you see a stock price dropping and know that a typically skittish fund is a large stockholder, it's safe to assume that the fund is dumping stock and that the price decline will continue.

Deep-value investors tend to buy on weakness, slowly accumulating stock through a patient, long-term process. Tweedy, Browne, for instance, is one such investor. An investor who sees Tweedy, Browne selling a rising stock can feel fairly confident that this move is likely due to a low cost basis. Deep-value investors often prudently trim portfolio positions as a price rises (due to their portfolio management philosophies), even when they see nothing wrong with an individual company.

ACTIVIST INVESTORS

Activist investors have a history of finding undervalued, underperforming companies and then pressuring underachieving management teams to make changes and deliver better returns. Hedge fund manager Carl Icahn, for instance, has a reputation for taking large, concentrated positions and then agitating for change.

In their paper "Hedge Funds as Shareholder Activists from 1994–2005," Northeastern University's Nicole Boyson and Robert Mooradian show that activist hedge funds did improve companies' operating performance. They concluded that

- Hedge funds are different from other types of activists. They rarely have the conflicts of interest (such as politically motivated agendas) that are common among pension and mutual funds. Hedge funds are willing to spend money. This research sample typically stayed active in target companies for more than two years, and may have lockup previsions that prevent fund investors from withdrawing money for a set time (usually six months to one year). This encourages longer-term strategies.
- Most mutual funds own no more than 5 percent of a company, but hedge funds can take concentrated positions of more than 10 percent. That compels management to take them more seriously.
- In their sample, the researchers say, "the risk-adjusted annual performance of hedge funds practicing aggressive activism and/or seeking changes in corporate governance is about 7 to 11 percent

higher than for nonactivist hedge funds and hedge funds pursuing less aggressive activism."

By following in the footsteps of activist hedge funds, an investor can benefit from their hard work.

FOOTPRINT TRACKING

StockPickr.com is a popular, comprehensive, and *free* resource for tracking 13F (fund holdings) 13D (activist, typically including a letter explaining what issues that stockholder has with management) and 13G (passive) filings. The Web site tracks the portfolios of different superstar investors, and shows other managers that also own a stock. It also tracks insider transactions. Set up a portfolio on the site, and it will list professional investors that are co-owners and send an alert when one of them makes a change. It's a good source of ideas and a starting point for fundamental research. One can also see 13G and 13D filings at www.sec.gov and www.yahoo.com/finance.

Stockpickr cofounder James Altucher describes the benefits of "piggybacking" on professional portfolios in his book *The Forever Portfolio*. The advantages include

- *Saving* millions in fees that superstar investors charge their clients. Notice if and when professionals buy or sell a stock, but do your own homework and make decisions that fit your needs and time frame.
- *Diversify* the scope of your sources. You can cherry-pick ideas from dozens of smart, sophisticated investors. A little research and experience will show which investors have an approach that fits your investment style and outlook.
- Find *expertise* in sectors such health care, banking, and technology, where it can be difficult to understand financial statements or competitive positioning. Niche funds employ specialists in these areas, and they can be a terrific resource for finding good companies in these sectors. Many funds publish occasional letters to investors that explain their outlook and rationale behind positions, or discuss their views with the financial press.

All-Time High List

It is one of the great paradoxes of the stock market that what seems too high usually goes higher and what seems too low usually goes lower.

—WILLIAM O'NEIL

Everyone loves a bargain. In the stock market, that often means trying to pick a bottom in a declining stock.

Some investors take a different approach. They focus on finding those few companies with a truly unique product or service and a ready market. The combination can translate into massive, sustainable, and underappreciated growth. These unique companies often hit all-time highs, because people with knowledge and money have aggressively purchased them. These investors have done their research, understand the company's unique qualities, and are willing to pay top dollar for the stock.

Trading dynamics change when a stock hits an all-time high. Traders who planned to sell when they broke even have already sold. Short sellers are showing a loss, adding to the stock's buying pressure if they decide to cover their short positions. It's hard to know when to sell these stocks, but total analyst acceptance or large secondary stock offerings can both offer clues. Remember that both up and down trends can last quite a while, as business conditions adjust and the public's mood fluctuates.

Investors interested in following trends should check out *Investor's Business Daily* (www.investors.com), which focuses on growth trends and companies showing sustainable operations and stock price momentum.

VENTURE CAPITALISTS

Ideas and ambition can only take a start-up company so far before it needs help from outside investors. Venture capitalists (VCs) fund start-ups, help them grow, and exit investments via a buyout or IPO. They look for big sustainable trends that their nascent companies can tap into. The two Stanford students who founded Google had a better approach to Internet search; their first VCs (Kleiner Perkins and Sequoia Capital) invested $25 million and owned nearly 10 percent of the company at the IPO. VCs expect that most of their funded companies will fail or break even. The occasional home run carries portfolio performance.

An awareness of the types of companies VCs are funding can lend insight into which trends VCs feel offer the most opportunity. It suggests that public companies in the same space may be good investments, particularly if they tap into the same or a similar market.

PRIVATE EQUITY

Private equity firms also invest in companies they believe they can improve and resell. Traditionally, they accept investor money from institutions and a few wealthy individuals, then use bank borrowing to buy small- and medium-sized companies. They aggressively manage the operations and then sell the firm to another private equity firm, a privately held company, or public company; they may also choose to take the company public via an IPO. Their success has attracted significant assets, which a private equity company must typically put to work within five years. Despite a difficult economic and investment environment, assets under management at private equity rose 15 percent, to $2.5 trillion, in 2008.

Some of the very brightest investors are at private equity firms, where they are somewhat immune from daily market pressures. They earn a management fee (usually 1 percent) and a bonus based on portfolio performance over time. Private equity firms don't often buy publicly traded companies, but they do sometimes make investments in publicly held firms.

It's not always possible or desirable to invest in the same company a private equity fund buys, especially as many of these firms are privately held, and may employ deal structures that a retail investor can't imitate. But smart investors can notice the industries and sectors that attract private equity money, and make portfolio decisions accordingly.

Buyer Beware

Don't overestimate the skill and wisdom of professionals.
—PETER LYNCH, former manager of the Fidelity Magellan Fund

Hobbyist golfers might take a certain satisfaction in watching golfing great Tiger Woods slice a tee shot deep into the woods. If asked, though, Woods would likely say that the muffed shot wasn't an accident—it was the result of a fundamental mistake, one that made that swing different from other, more successful shots.

Like great golfers, even the best investors make mistakes. The good ones try to discover the fundamental errors behind their goofs. Observers can, too.

BEATING THE BENCHMARK

Much of investing comes down to good judgment, patience, and diligent homework, which are difficult qualities for an outsider to measure. But an outsider can measure whether a manager is beating a stated benchmark, such as the S&P 500.

Underperforming a fund's benchmark can be a professional liability. As a result, many money managers obsess over their performance relative to their benchmark. They tend to follow market trends, trying to achieve performance that's as near the benchmark as possible. As European Central Bank President Jean-Claude Trichet said in a 2001 speech, "Some operators have come to the conclusion that it is better to be wrong along with everyone else, rather than take the risk of being right, or wrong, alone."

In a 2006 paper titled "The Price of Conformism," London School of Economics researchers Amil Dasgupta, Andrea Prat, and Michela Verardo examined U.S. fund manager filings from 1983 to 2004 to see which stocks were persistently bought and sold each quarter. The study found that

1. "On average, a strategy that buys stocks sold by institutions for five quarters and shorts stocks bought by institutions over the same period yields a cumulative market-adjusted return of 8 percent over one year and 17 percent after two years."
2. "We find about three quarters of institutions display conformist trading behavior . . . suggesting that our aggregate results are due to a generalized conformist tendency rather than few extreme outliers."

This study suggests that investors can profit by noticing consensus moves and considering whether these trends are supported by their merits, or occurring because professional investors are reluctant to stray from their peer group.

BILLIONAIRES ARE PEOPLE, TOO

George Soros is best known for his audacious macro bets, such as the $1 billion he made by "breaking the pound" in 1992. Soros had a knack for understanding breaking points; in this case, he recognized the limits of the British government's strategy to protect exchange rates by using government reserves to buy British currency that everyone else was trying to unload. The bet was complicated and nuanced, but backed by Soros's detailed homework, unmatched contacts and references, and patient timing.

Soros lost money, however, when he bought 9.5 million shares of Lehman Brothers in 2008, at an average $37.42 per share. Lehman announced bankruptcy September 14, 2008. It's not known just how much Soros lost on the trade. (Despite the loss, his fund reported a gain for 2008.)

Joseph Lewis, a legendary currency trader and friend of Bear Stearns then-CEO Jimmy Cayne, also lost money on banks. He amassed a $1.2 billion Bear Stearns stake (nearly half of his estimated $2.5 billion fortune) at an average price of $107 per share. On March 17, 2008, Bear Stearns was forcibly sold to J.P. Morgan, ultimately for $10 per share.

Even the Oracle of Omaha himself, Warren Buffett, makes mistakes. In 2008, early in his warnings of the dangers of derivatives and their potential harm to the banking sector, Buffett spent $244 million for shares of two Irish banks that appeared cheap to him. At year-end, his company wrote those holdings down to market: $27 million, for an 89 percent loss. "The tennis crowd would call my mistakes 'unforced errors,'" Buffet said in that year's letter to investors.

Outside investors should remember that no one is perfect.

SPECIALISTS WITHOUT PERSPECTIVE

Do portfolios fare better when managers have in-depth, specialized knowledge, or do generalist deliver superior results? We've discussed the benefits of following specialists. It is important to remember, too, that those who focus on a narrow topic can lose sight of larger factors. They don't see the forest for the trees.

N+1 magazine's interview with an unnamed hedge fund manager (HFM) in early 2008 makes that point. The manager and others looked around during 2006 and 2007, noticing the growing imbalances in the housing and lending markets. Surely, they felt, a day of reckoning would come. Among other holdings, the fund held mortgage-backed securities; the lead portfolio manager was concerned that this was a losing position. However, the staff mortgage expert assured the group that their mortgage securities were in good shape. The interviewer asked the obvious question about the in-house expert.

> **n+1**: When he saw the cranes in Florida, when he saw the commercials on TV, what did he think?
>
> **HFM**: I think his view was, the people who were predicting a crash in subprime were not experts in the subprime market. They were guys just basing their conclusions on anecdotal evidence. "But look, I'm knee deep in the data, I see the remittance reports every month, I've been involved in the 2003 subprime issuance, and the 2004 subprime issuance, and people said that stuff was dodgy, but it's performed very well. And I know all the details. You have anecdotes? I have details."
>
> And in equilibrium, yeah, if I tried to pick out of the mortgage pool which one is good and which one is bad based on having seen some cranes in Florida and hearing some stories about people taking out loans—
>
> **n+1**: —at a bar—
>
> **HFM**: Yeah, I had a conversation at a bar. This guy told me he was making a ton of money flipping houses. You know, you're not going to become a mortgage trader based on that. But you might catch the paradigm shift. So this guy was really, you know, he was very much at the detail level, and missed the paradigm shift.
>
> **n+1**: And now he's gone.
>
> **HFM**: And now he will have plenty of time to think about the big picture.

LIQUIDATIONS AND REDEMPTIONS

Good opportunities can come from understanding buying and selling pressures within the market. Every financial institution has times of stress, and these can lead to forced sales and purchases.

Distressed-bond funds receive new equity during a bankruptcy proceeding and are forced by their bylaws to sell the stock when it starts trading—they're a *bond* fund, after all. Index funds have to sell when a stock is deleted from their index, regardless of its underlying intrinsic value. Some mutual funds have bylaws forbidding owner-ship of stocks trading under $5 or $10 and are forced to sell if the price closes under that arbitrary level. Many brokerage firms won't allow margin credit on low-priced stocks, so anyone carrying a mar-gin balance may have to sell if a stock price declines. Some bond managers are required to only keep investment-grade bonds; they face an automatic sell if a company's bonds are downgraded.

These and other forced buying and selling scenarios provide opportunity. For instance, a trader may buy a stock right after an announcement that it will be included in the S&P 500 in just a few days. Index fund buying will likely push up the stock's price. (The market figures these things out quickly, though, so move fast.) Long-er-term investors may want to sell into the demand created by this forced purchase, even though it has nothing to do with company fundamentals. If the stock was approaching full valuation, a push from index funds is a gift. Many times the best opportunities come from understanding buying and selling imbalances, not from trying to make the best forecasts of future cash flows or liquidation values.

RESOURCES

Sources of private equity deals include www.thedeal.com (which also covers other categories such as mergers and acquisitions and bankruptcies) and www.pehub.com.

Sources for the actions and outlooks of venture capitalists include www.avc.com, www.venturebeat.com, and www.gigaom.com.

Among blogs, Market Folly (www.marketfolly.com) often discusses portfolio changes among well-regarded institutional funds. Alphaclone is a service that tracks institutional portfolio changes and has a blog at http://blog.alphaclone.com.

Long-time money manager Joel Greenblatt wrote on finding situations of forced buying and selling in his book *You Can Be a Stock Market Genius*.

Conclusion

Nothing endures but change.

—Heraclitus (Greek philosopher)

THIS BOOK would have been slightly different if written two years ago or a few years *from* now. Some investor behavior is timeless; other predictable patterns break down as markets adapt and change. Investors need a healthy degree of vigilance, a desire to understand the dominant trends and themes of the day, and enough humility to admit that no one ever knows it all. The markets will always contain a large element of chance.

What's more, there's no one right way to trade, whether you like instincts or systems, short-term or long-term trades, growth or value. Every investor needs to find a comfortable style.

You have to know what you are, and not try to be what you're not. If you are a day trader, day-trade. If you are an investor, then be an investor. It's like a comedian who gets up on stage and starts singing. What's he singing for? He's a comedian.

—STEVE COHEN, in *Stock Market Wizards*

Plenty of smart, generous traders and investors share their views via the media and blogosphere. The key is to cut through the clutter, find an approach that makes sense, and forge ahead.

I've always been a sucker for lists that help boil down the essence of a well-considered market approach. Dennis Gartman, who has written *The Gartman Letter* daily since 1987, has his own "Not-So-Simple Rules of Trading." These rules can be found on the Internet in short form, or in John Mauldin's book *Just One Thing,* where Gartman lays out his rules in expanded form.

Legendary investor John Templeton had his own list of "22 Principles for Successful Investing," which starts with my favorite: "There is only one long-term investment objective: maximum total after tax return."

Every professional, of course, has personal rules. Here are some of mine.

1. Keep it Simple. Ray Kroc, who built McDonald's into a global power, said that KISS ("Keep it simple, Stupid.") was his first founding principle for the young company. If you're looking for your investment rationale on the twentieth page of a spreadsheet, chances are it won't go as well as planned. My best success has come when an investment was plainly obvious.

2. "The intelligent man finds almost everything ridiculous, the sensible man hardly anything." (Goethe) Understand motivations, incentives, and pressures, and formerly questionable acts and outcomes begin to make sense.

3. "There's never just one cockroach in the kitchen." (Warren Buffett) Known as the cockroach theory, if you see one problem there is a good chance that others are lurking out of view. Don't wait for the second bug to appear. And don't trust someone who has lied or cheated. They've likely done it before and they will do it again.

4. "Believe none of what you hear and half of what you see." (Benjamin Franklin) Skepticism may not make you the life of the party, but will help your investment returns over time.

5. In a normal year, there is at least one time when the market becomes irrationally unglued (sometimes the market becomes *rationally* unglued). Many of the indicators in this book can help confirm gut feeling in finding this time.

6. Look for the downside first, the worst-case outcome of any given decision. The upside will take care of itself.

7. "A fool with a plan can beat a genius with no plan." (T. Boone Pickens) Writing down an investment's merits and drawbacks helps foster better decision making. Write down the reasons you would sell (or cover) a position before you buy.

8. Ego is expensive.

9. "Make everything as simple as possible, but not simpler." (Albert Einstein) If there's a danger in this book, it's that it may introduce too much thinking and complexity. Take what you can use and let the rest go by.

10. "Invert, always invert." (Charlie Munger, crediting mathematician Carl Jacobi) When faced with a tough problem, invert the problem (or situation) and look at it from another point of view. In terms of investing, it can mean challenging your assumptions and seeking out alternative and opposing views.

11. "When the facts change, I change my mind. What do you do, sir?" (John Maynard Keynes) Experts with strong, absolute views make good sound bites but often have a hard time changing their strong public stance when circumstances change. Investors with an open mind and nuanced opinions tend to make better decisions.

12. "When in doubt, don't." (Benjamin Franklin) It's fine to do nothing when there is nothing to do.

13. "Patience has its limits. Take it too far, and it's cowardice." (Holbrook Jackson) But you can't sit forever. At some point, you'll need to put capital at risk if you want your wealth to outpace inflation.

14. "You have to have a view. You can't be agnostic. But the big picture is not the way you make money. You look for individual opportunities." (James Grant) You need a view of sentiment cycles, the economy, and the current political winds. But it's equally important to turn over rocks and look for good individual investments. The two usually interact, with many compelling investments appearing at times when your big picture view suggests it's time for action.

15. "Lighten up, Francis." (Sergeant Hulka in *Stripes*) Turn off the television, go for a walk, play with the kids. It's easy to get caught up in the twenty-four-hour, hyperkinetic news cycle and succumb to the pressure to feel you're fully informed. It's not possible, and it's counterproductive. The most successful investors I know live balanced lives.

16. "This too shall pass." (King Solomon) When you're in the middle of a ripsnorting bull market, it seems that good news and rising stock prices will last indefinitely. The nastiest bear markets seem to bring unending gloom. But everything runs in

cycles, an axiom that's especially true for the stock market. The figure below offers perspective and acts as a reminder of the emotions at play during a normal market cycle. In its spot on my office wall, it helps me decide what to do next in a wide variety of market circumstances. I hope the indicators in this book do the same for you.

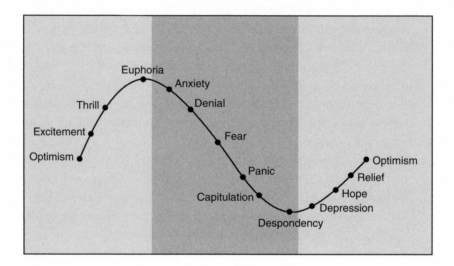

Figure C.1   The Investor Sentiment Cycle

Notes

CHAPTER 1   CLUES FROM THE OPTIONS MARKET

Find the white paper on the VIX and its composition at http://www.cboe.com/micro/vix/vixwhite.pdf.

Robert Whaley first introduced the term *investor fear gauge* in "The Investor Fear Gauge," a 2000 article in the *Journal of Portfolio Management*. The CBOE also credits him with developing the VIX in 1993.

Find "Implied Volatility and Future Portfolio Returns" at http://papers.ssrn.com/sol3/papers.cfm?abstract_id=896704.

Find "Can the VIX Signal Market Direction?" at http://papers.ssrn.com/sol3/papers.cfm?abstract_id=996384.

Find "Short-Term Declines in the VIX" "An Asymmetric Dynamic Strategy." at http://bespokeinvest.typepad.com/bespoke/2008/04/short-term-decl.html.

Bloomberg users should note to use VIXV. The CBOE issued a white paper with details on the composition of the VXV and its historical relationship to the VIX. Find a white paper introducing the VXV, "CBOE S&P 500 3-Month Volatility Index Description," at http://www.cboe.com/micro/vxv/3monthvix.pdf.

Find the academic paper "What Does Individual Option Volatility Smirk Tell Us about Future Equity Returns?" at http://papers.ssrn.com/sol3/papers.cfm?abstract_id=1107464.

Brett Steenbarger outlined his adjusted put/call ratio in a December 13, 2007, post at his http://traderfeed.blogspot.com blog titled "Spikes in the Equity Put/Call Ratio: A Signal With an Impressive Track Record," which can be found at http://traderfeed.blogspot.com/2007/12/spikes-in-equity-putcall-ratio-signal.html.

The Leuthold Weeden brief is from *Barron's* MarketWatch section, February 21, 2006.

CHAPTER 2   BIG MONEY ON THE MOVE

Hedge funds assets are discussed in a MarketWatch.com story of January 13, 2009, at http://www.marketwatch.com/news/story/industry-assets-fell-more-1-trillion-in-2008.

At the end of 2006, global financial assets managed by private institutional investors was $62 trillion. Go to http://www.ustreas.gov/offices/international-affairs/economic-exchange-rates/pdf/Dec-2007Appendix1.pdf.

A Jeffrey Saut strategy commentary of March 10, 2008, titled "Monkey See, Monkey Do" covers Lowry's analysis of 90 percent down days. Find Saut's weekly outlook for Raymond James at http://www.raymondjames.com/inv_strat.htm.

A two-part interview in February 2006 between Lowry president Paul Lowry and market commentator Barry Ritholtz on TheStreet.com, titled "Q&A: Paul Desmond of Lowry's Reports," covers Lowry's examination of market tops (among other topics). Go to http://www.thestreet.com/story/10269345/qa-paul-desmond-of-lowrys-reports.html.

Find Joel Ramin's January 2000 interview with Paul Tudor Jones titled "Interview with Paul Tudor Jones II) at http://chinese-school.netfirms.com/Paul-Tudor-Jones-interview.html.

Mebane Faber's commentary on volatility appeared in an August 7, 2008, blog post titled "Dow 300 Point Days and Volatility Clustering" at http://www.mebanefaber.com/2008/08/07/dow-300-point-days-and-volatility-clustering.

Find information on CalPERS at www.calpers.ca.gov.

CHAPTER 3   FAST MONEY ON THE MOVE

Find "Reasons to Fire Your Financial Adviser" by Chuck Jaffe, posted on April 15, 2008, at http://www.marketwatch.com/news/story/reasons-to-fire-your-financial-adviser?dist=msr_5.

CHAPTER 4   FOLLOW THE MONEY: CASH, DEBT, AND SHORTS

Jason Goepfert's paper "Mutual Fund Cash Reserves, the Risk-Free Rate and Stock Market Performance" won the 2004 Charles H. Dow award given by the Market Technicians Association. Download this paper at http://www.mta.org/eweb/docs/2004DowAwardRevised.pdf.

Sumner Redstone's sale of Midway stake is chronicled in the December 1, 2008, *Wall Street Journal* story "Redstone Sells Control of Midway to Ease Debt." Go to http://online.wsj.com/article/SB122810340075068473.html.

CHAPTER 5   TOO FAR, TOO FAST

A discussion of Lowry's 2007 study on the percentage of stocks above their 10-day moving average can be found in a March 12, 2007, blog entry titled "Latest correction—interesting stat from Lowry's" at http://trinityasset.blogspot.com/2007/03/latest-correction-interesting-stat-from.html.

Dick Arms's short column "More About the Arms Index" was published online at thestreet.com on February 13, 2003, and can be found at http://www.thestreet.com/p/rmoney/dickarms/10068127.html .Stockcharts.com outlines the ARMS index in their ChartSchool tab at http://stockcharts.com/school/doku.php?id=chart_school:technical_indicators:trin.

CHAPTER 6   RELATIVE VALUE

Federal Reserve economist staffers Joel Lander, Athanasios Orphanides, and Martha Douvogiannis's paper "Earnings, Forecasts, and the Predictability of Stock Returns: Evidence from Trading the S&P" investigates the relationship between forecasted earnings and bond yields and appeared in the Summer 1997 issue of the *Journal of Portfolio Management*.

John Hussman's August 20, 2007, commentary on the Fed Model is at http://hussmanfunds.com/wmc/wmc070820.htm.

David Merkel's blog post (alephblog.com) outlining his alternative to the Fed model is at http://alephblog.com/2007/07/09/the-fed-model.

Mark Hulbert looked into the history and efficacy of Value Line's Median Appreciation Potential (VLMAP) in an October 20, 2008, article on marketwatch.com titled "VLMAP to Wealth?" Go to http://www.marketwatch.com/story/last-time-this-market-timing-indicator-was-more-bullish-was-1982.

Find Henry Blodget's discussion of Shiller's cyclically adjusted price/earnings (CAPE) ratio in a January 9, 2009 blog post titled "Hallelujah: Stocks Finally Undervalued (Shiller)" at http://www.businessinsider.com/2009/1/hallelujah-stocks-finally-undervalued-shiller. Data in the chart were excerpted from Robert Shiller's Web site, www.irrationalexuberance.com. A variety of data and links to other information can be found at this online repository backing Shiller's well-known book *Irrational Exuberance*.

The 2001 and 2009 *Fortune* articles mentioning Warren Buffett and the ratio of market value to GNP were in "Warren Buffett on the Stock Market" by Warren Buffett and Carol J. Loomis at http://money.cnn.com/magazines/fortune/fortune_archive/2001/12/10/314691/ and "Buffett's Metric Says It's Time to Buy" by Carol J. Loomis and Doris Burke at http://money.cnn.com/2009/02/04/magazines/fortune/buffett_metric.fortune/index.htm.

CHAPTER 7   SENTIMENT SURVEYS

The August 2007 Merrill Lynch survey titled "Fund Managers Reluctant to Abandon Equities Amid Market Turbulence" is at http://www.ml.com/index.asp?id=769 5_7696_8149_74412_80983_81335.

CHAPTER 8   ANALYZING THE ANALYSTS

Peter Robison documents the pressure to produce smooth earnings streams in an April 22, 2008, article titled "What's an Analyst Worth? Not a Penny as Estimates Miss" at http://www.bloomberg.com/apps/news?pid=20601110&sid=apQUkLyvX WSA.

Professor Rajgopal's 2005 survey, conducted with John Graham (Duke University) and Campbell Harvey (National Bureau of Economic Research), was included in a paper titled "The Economic Implications of Corporate Financial Reporting," available at http://papers.ssrn.com/sol3/papers.cfm?abstract_id=491627.

The Duke/CFO Magazine Global Business Outlook Survey is at www.cfosurvey .org.

Wired magazine profile of Henry Blodget by Daniel Roth titled "Reinventing Henry" can be found at http://www.wired.com/techbiz/people/magazine/16-12/ ff_blodget.

"Buy-Side vs. Sell-Side Analysts' Earnings Forecasts" can be found at http://www .cfapubs.org/doi/pdfplus/10.2469/faj.v64.n4.3.

The Ned Davis Research insight that the historical market multiple trough earnings is 18.8 was disclosed in a November 28, 2008, research note by Ned Davis titled "More on Cheap Valuations and Good News on Inflation."

CHAPTER 9   REPORTING THE FINANCIAL NEWS, GAUGING THE INVESTOR'S PSYCHE

"Are Cover Stories Effective Contrary Indicators?" by Tom Arnold, John Earl, and David North (University of Richmond) can be downloaded at http://www.cfapubs .org/doi/pdf/10.2469/faj.v63.n2.4520.

The Time covers for the June 2005 story on housing and 1999 story on Amazon's Jeff Bezos appear at http://www.time.com/time/covers/0,16641,20050613,00.html and http://www.time.com/time/covers/0,16641,19991227,00.html.

Barry Ritholtz's comment on a bullish front-page Wall Street Journal story appeared in a May 23, 2007, post titled "Uh-Oh: Front Page WSJ "Why Market Optimists Say This Bull Has Legs." Go to http://bigpicture.typepad.com/comments/2007/05/ uhoh_front_page.html.

A *Globe and Mail* column by Derek DeCloet titled "Don Coxe Insisted Commodity Prices Would Keep Rising. Then Came the Crash" profiled Donald Coxe on February 19, 2009. Go to http://www.theglobeandmail.com/report-on-business/don-coxe-insisted-commodity-prices-would-keep-rising-then-came-the-crash/article9506.

Jon Stewart's October 2008 mocking of CNBC's "decabox" was posted at Paul Kedrosky's well-followed "Infectious Greed" blog at http://paul.kedrosky.com/. The link to that post is http://paul.kedrosky.com/archives/2008/10/14/the_decabox_mak.html.

CHAPTER 10   SITTING AND WATCHING

Find the "Gone Fishing—Seriously" post on Footnoted.org of November 25, 2008, at http://www.footnoted.org/perk-city/gone-fishing-seriously.

Notes on Jim Chanos commenting on shorting in general and his involvement in Enron can be found in a speech given at a SEC roundtable discussion at http://www.sec.gov/spotlight/hedgefunds/hedge-chanos.htm.

Find the Schlumberger layoff story outlined in the January 8, 2009 *Wall Street Journal* article titled "Schlumberger Cuts Signal Longer Slump in Energy Industry" at http://online.wsj.com/article/SB123145200537165687.htm.

Find Google's analyst conference call of July 17, 2008 at http://seekingalpha.com/article/85608-google-inc-q2-2008-earnings-call-transcript?page=1. Note that seekingalpha.com provides many conference call transcripts for free.

Ian Austen chronicled the SEC finding on Biovail was chronicled in a March 25, 2008, *New York Times* article, "U.S. and Canada Accuse Drug Maker of Fraud," available at http://www.nytimes.com/2008/03/25/business/25biovail.html.

The *Wall Street Journal* published a page-one article titled "Whole Foods is Hot, Wild Oats a Dud—So Said 'Rahodeb'" on July 12, 2007, outlining Whole Foods CEO John Mackey's Yahoo message posting under an anonymous moniker. Go to http://online.wsj.com/article/SB118418782959963745.html.

Herb Greenberg's column on Starbuck's CEO Howard Schultz "Schultz at Starbucks: Chief Exec of the Decade?" was on MarketWatch.com on December 13, 2004. Go to http://www.marketwatch.com/story/shultz-at-starbucks-chief-exec-of-the-decade.

Download "Where Are the Shareholders' Mansions? CEOs' Home Purchases, Stock Sales, and Subsequent Company Performance" by Crocker Liu (Arizona State) and David Yermack (New York University) at http://papers.ssrn.com/sol3/papers.cfm?abstract_id=970413&download=yes.

The Reuter's story by Michael Flaherty titled "Blackstone CEO Gala Sign of Buyout Boom" on Stephen Schwarzman's sixtieth birthday party is at http://www .reuters.com/article/mergersNews/idUSN1440877020070214.

Details about the proceeds generated by the Blackstone IPO appeared in a February 11, 2008, profile in *The New Yorker* by James B. Stewart titled "The Birthday Party." Find it at http://www.newyorker.com/reporting/2008/02/11/080211fa_fact_ stewart.

Bloomberg.com recapped Dennis Kozlowski's time as Tyco's CEO and the divorce petition by Karen Kozlowski in a August 16, 2006, story titled "Wife of Ex-Tyco Chief Kozlowski Files for Divorce." Find it at http://www.bloomberg.com/apps/ news?pid=20601103&sid=a.b2pBWuZEJY&refer=us.

David Gaffen's November 21, 2008, post in the *Wall Street Journal*'s MarketBeat blog titled "Skyscrapers to Recessions" gives an overview of global skyscrapers as a precursor sign of a top. Go to http://blogs.wsj.com/marketbeat/2008/11/21/ skyscrapers-to-recessions.

Chris Isidore of *Money* magazine has written a few times about the curse of stadium-naming deals, including "Stadium Curse Still Haunts Firms" on February 3, 2003 (http://money.cnn.com/2003/01/03/commentary/column_sportsbiz/ sponsor_stock_index) and "A Stadium Name Bubble?" on January 21, 2007 (http://money.cnn.com/2007/01/19/commentary/sportsbiz/index.htm).

Floyd Norris' *New York Times* column of January 12, 2000, titled "Media Megadeal," chronicled the Time Warner-America Online merger. Find it at http://www .nytimes.com/2000/01/12/business/media-megadeal-market-place-two-stocks- one-swings-the-other-doesn-t.html.

Scott Moritz discussed eBay's purchase of Skype in TheStreet.com story of September 13, 2005, titled "eBay Believes the Skype." Find it at http://www.thestreet .com/_rms/tech/scottmoritz/10242194.html.

Coca-Cola's time as owner of Columbia Pictures is chronicled as part of the long history of Columbia at filmsite.org (http://www.filmsite.org/milestones1980s. html). Columbia's sale to Sony Pictures in 1989 was documented in a November 28, 1994, *Time* magazine article titled "So Many Dreams So Many Losses." Go to http://www.time.com/time/magazine/article/0,9171,981894,00.html.

John Rothchild recounted the "shoe shine boy" story in an April 16, 1996, story in *Fortune* magazine titled "When the shoeshine boys talk stocks it was a great sell signal in 1929," available found at http://money.cnn.com/magazines/fortune/ fortune_archive/1996/04/15/211503/index.htm

CHAPTER 11   THE INSIDERS

Go to http://money.cnn.com/2002/04/25/pf/investing/grubman to read Amy Feldman and Joan Caplin's article "Is Jack Grubman the Worst Analyst Ever?" published in *Money*, April 25, 2002.

Download "How Informative Are Analyst Recommendations and Insider Trades?" by Jim Hsieh (George Mason University), Lilian Ng (University of Wisconsin, Milwaukee), and Qinghai Wang (Georgia Institute of Technology) at http://papers.ssrn.com/sol3/papers.cfm?abstract-id=687584.

Matt Krantz documented the insider selling within the homebuilding sector in an October 5, 2006, article titled "Home Builders' CEOs Make Timely Stock Sales" in *USA Today*. Find it at http://www.usatoday.com/money/economy/housing/2006-10-04-builder-sell-usat_x.htm.

Paul Krugman's *New York Times* October 1, 2007, column titled "Enron's Second Coming" outlined the Countrywide buyback and stock sales by then-CEOs Anthony Mozilo. Go to http://www.nytimes.com/2007/10/01/opinion/01krugman.html.

Stanford professor Alan Jagolinzer's study "Do Insiders Trade Strategically within the SEC Rule 10b5-1 Safe Harbor?" can be downloaded at content.lawyerlinks.com/library/sec/misc/articles/10b51%20stanford%20paper.pdf

Gradient's research into 10b5-1 plans was discussed in a *Wall Street Journal* article by Ed Welsch titled "Trading Plans Offer a Good Clue to Sell" on April 9, 2008, page C4. Go to http://online.wsj.com/article/SB120770890145300645.html.

Jane Sasseen documented Jagolinzer's study and Broadcom CEO McGregor's selling in a *BusinessWeek* article titled "Insiders with a Curious Edge," published on December 7, 2006. Go to http://www.businessweek.com/bwdaily/dnflash/content/dec2006/db20061206_457919.htm.

CHAPTER 12   LOOKING TO THE FUTURES

Harvard and Yale endowment allocations to commodities in 1990 is outlined in James Stewart's article "A League of Their Own" in the September 2007 *SmartMoney* magazine, available at http://www.smartmoney.com/investing/mutual-funds/a-league-of-their-own-21880.

Forbes looked into the troubles Harvard's endowment was experiencing in early 2009 with a March 16, 2009, cover piece titled "Harvard: The Inside Story of Its Finance Meltdown" by Bernard Condon and Nathan Vardi, available at http://www.forbes.com/forbes/2009/0316/080_harvard_finance_meltdown.html.

CFTC trading exemptions can be found at http://www.cftc.gov/industryoversight/intermediaries/cpoctaexemptionsexclusions.html.

A March 11, 2009, *Wall Street Journal* article titled "CFTC to Review Hedge-Exemption Rules" outlined the state of CFTC review in early 2009 into the exemptions allowing traders to exceed speculative position limits. Go to http://online.wsj.com/article/SB123682272262803693.html.

CHAPTER 13   GIVING CREDIT TO THE BOND MARKET

A good a review of the TED spread is available at http://www.liborated.com/libor_news01_31_09.asp.

Download the academic study "Predicting the Bear Stock Market: Macroeconomic Variables as Leading Indicators" by Shiu-Sheng Chen of National Taiwan University at http://papers.ssrn.com/sol3/papers.cfm?abstract_id=1106100.

David Evans wrote a profile of the CDS market ("The Risk Nightmare") in the July 2008 issue of *Bloomberg Magazine*, posted at http://www.bloomberg.com/apps/news?pid=20601109&refer=home&sid=aCFGw7GYxY14).

The CDS data on the financial and housing sectors is from Bloomberg.

CHAPTER 14   MONEY IN, MONEY OUT

One basic tutorial on initial public offerings can be found at www.investopedia.com/university/ipo.

Templeton's shorting of pending IPO lockups was among other classic trades profiled in a December 16, 2004, article in *The Economist* titled "Why Didn't I Think of That?" Go to http://www1.economist.com/research/articlesBySubject/displaystory.cfm?subjectid=682272&story_id=E1_PQJDGVQ.

Sprott Inc.'s IPO was profiled in a May 15, 2008, article on Bloomberg.com titled "Sprott Falls in Trading Debut after C$200 Million IPO," available at http://www.bloomberg.com/apps/news?pid=20601082&sid=aNXIiDtSLIW8&refer=canada.

Eric Falkenstein ("Falkenblog" at falkenblog.blogspot.com) highlights National City's secondary offering in an April 22, 2008, blog post titled "Confounding Indicator: Bank Capital Issuance" at http://falkenblog.blogspot.com/2008/04/confounding-indicator-bank-capital.html.

Michael Shedlock mentions the secondary offerings from TBS International and Genko Shipping on Mish's Global Economic Trend Analysis in a post titled "Secondary Offerings, Debt, and Defaults" at http://globaleconomicanalysis.blogspot.com/2008/05/seconday-offerings-debt-and-defaults.html.

T. Boone Pickens was featured in a Time magazine cover story on March 4, 1985 titled "High Times for T. Boone Pickens". His pursuit of Gulf Oil is one of many profiled deals. The story can be found at http://www.time.com/time/magazine/article/0,9171,961946,00.html.

Jason Zweig wrote on buybacks in his Intelligent Investor column of August 30, 2008, titled "With Buybacks, Look Before You Leap" at http://online.wsj.com/article/SB122005273251785043.html.

Qualcomm buyback analysis from its 2006 annual report downloaded from the U.S. Securities and Exchange Commission's EDGAR database at www.sec.gov/edgar.shtml.

CHAPTER 15   TRACKING THE TRAILBLAZERS

Gerald Martin (American University) and John Puthenpurackal (University of Nevada, Las Vegas) studied the outperformance of a portfolio built around copying Warren Buffett's moves in their April 2008 paper "Imitation Is the Sincerest Form of Flattery: Warren Buffett and Berkshire Hathaway." Over the period from 1976 to 2006, a portfolio populated with stocks bought at the beginning of the month, after they were publicly disclosed, returned 10.75 percent over the S&P 500. Go to http://papers.ssrn.com/sol3/papers.cfm?abstract_id=806246.

"Hedge Funds as Shareholder Activists from 1994–2005" by Nicole Boyson (Northeastern University) and Robert Mooradian (Northeastern University) is available at http://papers.ssrn.com/sol3/papers.cfm?abstract_id=992739.

James Altucher's book *The Forever Portfolio* includes Chapter 15, "Piggybacking," in which he outlines the case for tracking the movements of some longer-term-oriented portfolio managers.

Amil Dasgupta, Andrea Prat, and Michela Verardo's paper "The Price of Conformism" is available at http://econ.lse.ac.uk/staff/prat/papers/dpv.pdf.

Private Equity trends were discussed in a February 23, 2009 story titled "Private Equity Assets Rise 15% in '08" at www.finalternatives.com/node/7036.

George Soros's position in Lehman was disclosed in August 2008 in a Reuters story published on August 15, 2008, titled "Soros Boosts Lehman Stake to 9.5 Million Shares" at http://www.reuters.com/article/innovationNews/idUSN 1449757120080815. Soros later penned a piece describing the roiling financial crisis of late 2008, in the *Financial Times* on January 28, 2009 ("The Game Changer"), in which he revealed his fund was up 10 percent in 2008. Go to http://www.ft.com/cms/s/0/49b1654a-ed60-11dd-bd60-0000779fd2ac.html.

A Time.com story, "Top 10 Worst Business Deals of 2008," outlined Joseph Lewis's loss on Bear Stearns. Go to http://www.time.com/time/specials/2008/top10/article/0,30583,1855948_1864555,00.html.

n+1 magazine published "Interview with a Hedge Fund Manager" on January 7, 2008, available at http://www.nplusonemag.com/interview-hedge-fund-manager.

CONCLUSION

The Investor's Anthology: Original Ideas from the Industry's Greatest Minds by Charles D. Ellis and James R. Vertin excerpts John Templeton's "22 Principles for Successful Investing."

Index

About Bloomberg

BLOOMBERG L.P., founded in 1981, is a global information services, news, and media company. Headquartered in New York, Bloomberg has sales and news operations worldwide.

Serving customers on six continents, Bloomberg, through its wholly-owned subsidiary Bloomberg Finance L.P., holds a unique position within the financial services industry by providing an unparalleled range of features in a single package known as the Bloomberg Professional® service. By addressing the demand for investment performance and efficiency through an exceptional combination of information, analytic, electronic trading, and straight-through-processing tools, Bloomberg has built a worldwide customer base of corporations, issuers, financial intermediaries, and institutional investors.

Bloomberg News, founded in 1990, provides stories and columns on business, general news, politics, and sports to leading newspapers and magazines throughout the world. Bloomberg Television, a 24-hour business and financial news network, is produced and distributed globally in seven languages. Bloomberg Radio is an international radio network anchored by flagship station Bloomberg 1130 (WBBR-AM) in New York.

In addition to the Bloomberg Press line of books, Bloomberg publishes *Bloomberg Markets* magazine.

To learn more about Bloomberg, call a sales representative at:

London: 144-20-7330-7500
New York: 11-212-318-2000
Tokyo: 181-3-3201-8900

About the Author

Richard Sipley is a senior portfolio manager at Boston Private Bank & Trust Company, where he manages investment portfolios for individuals and institutions. Sipley has more than fourteen years of experience as a senior portfolio manager. He holds an MBA with concentrations in finance and economics from the Kellogg School of Management at Northwestern University. He was certified as a Chartered Financial Analyst (CFA) in 1998. He lives in Andover, Massachusetts.

The author can be reached at rsipley@gmail.com.